MYTHS AND MYSTERIES
OF NORTH CAROLINA

True stories
of the unsolved and unexplained

Sara Pitzer

Guilford, Connecticut

Dedicated with respect to the storytellers who have gone before and with encouragement to those who will come next.

To buy books in quantity for corporate use
or incentives, call **(800) 962-0973**
or e-mail **premiums@GlobePequot.com.**

Image p. 48 © Edith F. Carter

Layout: Sue Murray
Project editor: Gregory Hyman
Maps by M.A. Dubé © Morris Book Publishing, LLC

Library of Congress Cataloging-in-Publication Data is available on file.

ISBN 978-0-7627-5983-5

Printed in the United States of America

10 9 8 7 6 5 4 3 2 1

CONTENTS

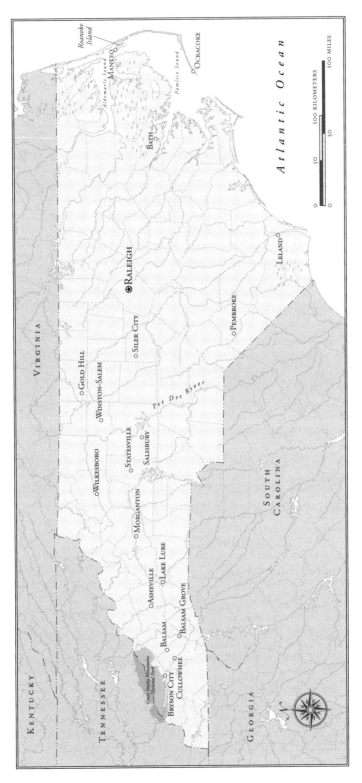

NORTH CAROLINA

ACKNOWLEDGMENTS

I have always wanted to write a book in which I said, "I'd thank everybody who helped me, but I did this all by myself." Well, it can't happen here. The number of people who provided information, suggestions, and support is long enough to be humbling.

First, I must thank Craig Distl, of Distl Public Relations. He specializes in tourism. Craig offered suggestions for chapters, provided research information I needed to write them, helped me get photographs, arranged interviews with pertinent people, took me with him on some of his trips so I could do interviews in person without driving alone to get there. Equally important, he shared information about places where he didn't even have clients. His help has made this a better book.

Reference librarians Melody Moxley and Betty Moore at the headquarter location of the Rowan County Library helped me through many months of research. They found sources and arranged interlibrary loans for obscure books.

At the Albemarle headquarters of the Stanly County Library, library assistant Pamela Arey did the same things.

I enjoyed working with my editor, Meredith Rufino, more than I can remember having enjoyed working with an editor before. She, too, answered lots of questions, offered guidance and reassurance, and when necessary, nudged me along to keep up with the publishing schedule. Moreover, she did it with great wit and good humor.

Chapter-by-Chapter

The Lost Colony

John Buford, in charge of media relations at The Lost Colony drama organization, solved the problem of illustrating a chapter about a community that isn't there anymore.

Historic Gold Hill

Many of the people who live in Gold Hill shared stories about their unexplained experiences there. Vivian Pennington-Hopkins explained how such experiences might relate to the old ghost stories.

Pee Dee A.D.

At this state historic site, where budget problems have reduced the staff, Rich Thompson, the site manager, took the time to offer his take on the kinds of questions such a place engenders. His was the interpretation that turned the story from merely historic to truly human.

Tsul 'Kalu and the Judaculla Rock

Julie Spiro, executive director of the Jackson County Chamber of Commerce and the Jackson County Travel and Tourism Authority, put me in touch with a source for one of the few good pictures that exist of the rock.

The Sad Tale of Tom Dula

Brandon McCann, executive director of the Cascade Highlands of North Carolina and Virginia, helped provide a picture of Tom Dula, whose appearance is unknown, by sending me a "portrait" painted by Edith F. Carter, who graciously allowed its reproduction in this book.

Blackbeard the Pirate

Jon and Marti Lakey gave over time during their trip to the coast celebrating their twentieth wedding anniversary so Jon could take pictures for this chapter.

Brown Mountain Lights

Practically every North Carolinian I talked to about work on this book said, "Are you writing about the Brown Mountain Lights?" I wouldn't have dared to skip that one.

Apparition at Maco Station

Eddie Howell talked with me about how paranormal investigators work and explained the background that led him to an interest in the activity.

The Devil's Tramping Ground

Neha M. Shah, director of travel and tourism for Pittsboro-Siler City CVB and Chatham County, brought me up to date on the condition of the barren circle and sent me to Dr. John Shillito, who has taken pictures reflecting its state in recent time.

The Ballad of Frankie Silver

Historian Elaine Dellinger showed me around the museum and offices of the Yancy County History Association. She shared with me various accounts of the Frankie Silver story and recommended sources for more information.

Theresa Phillips, of Legacy Films Ltd., also spoke with me at length about Frankie Silver. She provided me with a prerelease copy of a new special edition of her film, *The Ballad of Frankie Silver.* Her nontraditional interpretation of the story from the point of view of Frankie's daughter, Nancy, added a new dimension to the chapter.

Hospitality Haunts

My daughter, Lee Pitzer, told me stories about many haunted places around Asheville, and connected me with Jeannine Wynne, who was willing to drive off in all directions to take pictures of them.

The Legend of Cowee Tunnel

Kim Albritton, vice president and general manager of the Great Smoky Mountains Railroad, provided enough information about the history of railroads in Western North Carolina and the Cowee Tunnel to fill a book. Thanks to her, I've also ridden the train through that tunnel.

Strange Events at Old Salem

Jackson Boone not only took photographs for me in Old Salem but also wrote an account of what he saw during his time at the North Carolina Governor's School there. It demonstrated how some high school students experience the place in an age when technology competes with ghosts and legends for attention.

The Spirits of Salisbury

Daphne Safrit, manager of Literary Bookpost, an independent bookstore in Salisbury, provided me with almost a year's worth of running accounts about unexplained events in Salisbury, including her personal experiences.

INTRODUCTION

Some things can't be explained. In a sense, this entire book is based on that premise. But it must be human nature, when faced with what we don't know, to try to find, or create, explanations. So legends grow from how we explain to ourselves the things we don't understand. The legend of "Tsul 'Kalu and the Judaculla Rock" is a good example. Some of the giant's roaring, leaping from mountaintop to mountaintop in a rage, cursing braves who upset him, must be how early tribes of Cherokee people accounted for thunder, lightning, and bad luck hunting. It must also be human nature to keep looking for additional information as we do learn about the world. Today, with thunder and lightning pretty well understood, folks acknowledge that old legend as a story that's been passed down over generations, but they still want to explain the strange markings on the rock, since no giant actually etched them with his toenails. Such curiosity seems to lead us from one understanding into the next question. Somehow there is always a next question. Maybe that's why the old stories grow and change over time, to allow for new knowledge and point to the next related question. Think about it this way. Suppose someone finally proved, absolutely, that the markings were made by creatures from another planet.

Inevitably, the next generation of storytellers would try to figure out what planet they came from, why they were here, and why they didn't stay. They'd probably try to deduce the aliens' social structure and what they ate for supper as well. I believe that each generation of good storytellers adds knowledge to the old tales and introduces new questions.

Two of the writers whose work certainly influenced mine were Nancy Roberts and John Harden. They've both passed on to whatever comes after this life, but the volumes of their stories still stand prominently in our libraries. When I told people that I was working on this book, one of the most frequent questions was, "Are you the new Nancy Roberts?" No way. She was in a class by herself. Nancy Roberts (1924–2008) was a model of research and storytelling. I knew her personally, though not well, when my job was to market a book she'd written for the University of South Carolina Press. Over the years, she wrote more than two dozen books, most of which have been reprinted many times. She also spoke at schools frequently, exciting successive generations of children with her stories and talks. I learned from her that the old stories were never old to people reading and hearing them for the first time, and that each legend or mystery deserves to be taken seriously. I did not know John William Harden (1914–1986), but I wish I had. Living in Greensboro, he was a whirlwind of activity, too. He worked as a journalist and newspaper editor. He advised North Carolina governors and textile executives, and founded the state's first full-service public relations company. In writing old ghost stories, he practiced the journalistic deal—narrating the stories as they were told to him, without judgmental commentary. What stands out is the respect he had for the people who told him the tales.

I've certainly given those old legends and mysteries their due in telling here, but I've included some more recent events, too. These tend to fall into the category of ghost or paranormal activity, perhaps because they haven't had time yet to become legends. I don't think those chapters reflect my personal attitude toward such accounts. I'm not even sure exactly what it would be. Harden wrote that the longer he worked with the topic the more he seemed aware of presences. The notion of apparitions and such things always interested me, but I didn't want to participate. As a young woman, I kept a dish of pretzels by my bed to eat in case I had to get up in the middle of the night because I thought that was when apparitions appeared. I did not want to see any, and I figured nobody eating a pretzel ever did. It worked. I never have. However, my recent research leaves me convinced that intelligent, down-to-earth people have unexplained experiences that deserve attention. So you'll find some of their stories here, too, told, I hope, with the same respect John Harden would've granted them.

CHAPTER ONE

The Lost Colony

What would you think if, after being away several years, you returned to your favorite little village, where you knew everybody and expected a happy welcome, only to find the place deserted with no explanation of what had happened and no idea where to find your friends and relatives? And how long would you keep looking for them? That's the heart of what's become known as America's oldest mystery—the disappearance of the settlers on Roanoke Island sometime between 1587 and 1590.

The colony was just called "Roanoke" until the first performance of the outdoor drama *The Lost Colony* in 1937. Almost every summer since 1937, *The Lost Colony* has been performed at the Waterside Theater in Manteo, on Roanoke Island, dramatizing the unexplained disappearance of the English colony established in 1587 on the island, where Virginia Dare became the first English child to be born in the "new world." That appellation caught on and the little colony has been called "Lost" ever since. In a sense, the drama has become a local industry. Many of

PHOTO COURTESY ROANOAKE ISLAND HISTORICAL
ASSOCIATION, PRODUCERS OF *THE LOST COLONY*

Players in the outdoor drama *The Lost Colony* at Manteo depict a fictional version of how the colonists may have packed up to walk on to a safer place.

the town's residents have performed in it over the years, often in more than one role. Local people know this show well enough to recite lines by heart. What they don't know is how to explain the disappearance of ninety men, seventeen women, and eleven children, apparently without a struggle, sometime between 1587, when John White, the colony's governor and Virginia Dare's grandfather, left for England to get more supplies, and August 1590, when he finally returned.

What happened to the colonists? Do they have descendants and, if so, who and where are they? What took John White three years to get back to Roanoke Island? *The Lost Colony* drama is fiction, but it keeps the questions alive. And the longer people wonder, the more possible answers come along, none of them entirely adequate so far.

The mystery begins in the 1500s, when England was eager to establish a presence in other lands as Spain was already doing vigorously. Colonizers in those days didn't pay much attention to the fact that these "new" places were already populated, so Queen Elizabeth I, who ruled England at the time, gave Walter Raleigh permission to colonize in the New World. Also, he was supposed to set up a coastal base from which privateers (sanctioned pirates for the Crown) could launch raids against Spanish ships and bring home whatever valuables they might find, such as precious metal, to fill England's coffers. Of course the men who found these things would also profit, as would the sponsors of the colonies. Raleigh didn't go himself. First, in 1584, he sent an expedition with Philip Amadas and Arthur Barlowe to explore the Atlantic coast, looking for new sources of wealth. They landed on part of the area we now know as North Carolina's Outer Banks. It seemed a good place from which to attack Spanish settlements farther south and to introduce themselves to the local native tribes. In a search for appropriate sites of future colonization, Amadas and Barlowe explored the coast in the vicinity of Hatteras and then moved north to what may have been Roanoke Inlet. Accounts differ somewhat in descriptions of what happened when the expedition got to Roanoke Island. They apparently received pleasant welcomes and explored the area with native guides. Then they returned to England about a year later with two natives, Manteo and Wanchese, to parade around for a sort of show-and-tell in England. And they brought back to England reports of the agreeable climate, ample wildlife, and lush growth on the island—a land of plenty peopled by friendly and benevolent Indians. What's not to love? The queen gave Raleigh the right to all the land he could occupy and told him to name it "Virginia." The name stems from the fact that Elizabeth, having never married, was the virgin queen; its technical accuracy is not assured.

The next trip, Raleigh still didn't go himself. Instead, he sent about one hundred men, including craftsmen who could build and outfit a community on the island, scholars to study and write about it, and John White, an artist, to capture its images. But the group's leader, Ralph Lane, was a military man in an era when soldiers were accustomed to taking what they wanted and moving harshly against perceived slights. Also, it was too late in the season for the group to grow any food, and in the absence of women, stores probably were ill used, while some were spoiled in transport. Reports differ somewhat, but the actions of the men included kidnapping, killing a chief, burning his village and its crops over a supposedly stolen silver cup, perhaps raping a native woman, and treating the natives as "savages." It must have been confusing to the natives to have the English start out friendly, with John White drawing pictures of them, and then turn warlike. The natives became hostile in return. Today, the expedition's failure seems almost inevitable. A group of lonely, hungry men, with no idea when a supply ship might arrive, scared of attacks from natives they'd alienated with aggressive behavior, would want to get out of there and go home. So when Sir Francis Drake showed up at the island after plundering St. Augustine, Florida, the men climbed aboard and headed back to England. Ironically, a supply ship showed up just two weeks later. Its crew found only a deserted fort and some buildings, so they went on, leaving behind just fifteen men to maintain the English presence on the site. Today, scholars wonder why the English thought fifteen men would be safe in an area populated by many natives, most of whom no longer trusted the English.

Even though things had gone sour, Sir Walter Raleigh still wanted a colony in the New World. He tried again, this time with an assembled group of 117 men, women, and children to create a proper settlement. He made the artist, John White, governor. The group also included White's daughter, Eleanor, who was pregnant, and her husband, Annanias Dare, as well as the chief, Manteo. Again, today we wonder about the wisdom of sending people of high birth, who were accustomed to comfortable life in English society and had minimal skills, to start over in a place about which they knew little. And why were these new settlers willing to go? Raleigh had changed his mind about where to establish a settlement and tried to send the group to the Chesapeake Bay. But when the ship's pilot, Simon Fernandes, with the crew and settlers, stopped at Roanoke Island to pick up the fifteen men left behind a year before, the men were gone, except for some bones. The Croatoan natives, on what we know today as Hatteras Island, said the men had been attacked by other native tribes, though some had survived and sailed up the coast. Not a warm welcome. Fernandes insisted the colonists stay at Roanoke anyway because, as a privateer, he was itching to get into the war brewing between Spain and England and gather wealth, not ferry passengers to a new settlement site.

On Roanoke, Governor White tried to restore friendly relations with the native tribes that had been attacked earlier by Lane's men, but he wasn't successful. Not only would the colonists be on their own for food, but also they feared for their lives. Facing the threat of starvation as well as death, the colonists urged White to go back to England with Fernandes to get more supplies and recruit help. He must have left reluctantly, but in August 1587, just a month after the birth of his granddaughter, Virginia Dare, White sailed away with Fernandes, even though it was winter, a bad time for the trip. In an era well before electronic communication, the best White could do was to tell his colony to carve a Maltese cross on a tree if something happened and they had to leave.

Three years passed.

While published accounts of the settlement attempts to this point differ only in a few details, speculation about what took White so long to return varies considerably more. The usual explanation is that all England's ships were commandeered for the escalating war with Spain, but speculations hint at political manipulations, some of which are spelled out in "The Story at The Lost Colony Genealogy and DNA Research Group," at www.rootsweb.ancestry.com/~molcgdrg/faqs/lcstory.htm.

One contributor at this site, Roberta Estes, wrote that the story is ". . . like a large knit sweater, once you start to pull on one raveling, slowly the entire sweater starts to unravel, and eventually, that small raveling is much larger than you ever expected."

According to the classic story, when White was finally able to return to Roanoke, he found the place deserted, yet there was no sign of violence, nor any cross carved on a tree. Only the words "Croatoan" carved into a fort post and "Cro" on a tree gave any indication that the colonists might have tried to communicate. Moreover, the colonists had taken belongings with them, as if they hadn't run away in panic. At the time, the obvious conclusion was that they'd moved to Croatoan Island, but nobody tried to look for them because of a coming storm. So White sailed away, presumably with no idea what had happened to his family and colonists. Isn't that odd behavior for a father and grandfather? One researcher who searched original documents became convinced that perhaps he did know, and for political reasons chose not to tell. And Karen Ordahl Kupperman titled her book, published in 1984, *The Abandoned Colony.*

Today one persistent theory about the colonists is that they went to live with some of the native tribes, perhaps splitting up. Some of them might have decided to move on to Chesapeake Bay, where they'd originally expected to go, while others headed for Croatoan, and in both cases, were assimilated. Proponents point especially to the Lumbee people, now in Pembroke, North Carolina, whose features tend to be pale skinned, not resembling other tribes such as the Cherokees. Many Lumbees, too, believe they have ancestors from the Roanoke colony. (www.members .tripod.com/~redheart/thelostcolony.htm). This group of natives was never forced onto an Indian reservation. Similarly, Native Americans of Person County, North Carolina, were reported by later settlers to know English and, in some cases, to have "European" features. In a relatively new development, ongoing DNA testing (www.lost-colony.com/DNAproject.html) is in process to gather information scientifically. Their invitation says, "If your family descends from the Eastern Carolina area, if your family has an oral tradition of Lumbee or other Native American ancestry from the Eastern United States, or if your family includes one of our 'most wanted' surnames, join the Lost Colony DNA Project with Family Tree DNA." The surnames, from lists of colonists and "families of interest," begin with Allen and Bishop and range all the way through Waters and Wright. The project sponsors hope to learn what happened to the colonists as well as the early native population. Where did they go? Did they survive? If so, who are their descendants and where do they live today? This reflects a conviction that members of the first colony did survive and reproduce. Or perhaps native tribes took the colonists as slaves, using the women not only for labor but also sexual activity, which could also account for later changes in the physical characteristics of some natives and would allow for the possibility of descendants today.

A less hopeful theory is that the whole colony moved together and later all were killed, perhaps by the Spanish. But the Spanish actually had reported finding the remains of the deserted fort in 1588, and even if they'd resorted to mass slaughter, there'd have been remains.

Other possibilities that have surfaced include the colonists dying in an attempt to return to England on their own in vessels that were not seaworthy, and being victims of cannibalism. But who would take a baby onto the ocean in a small boat? And even cannibals leave behind bones. Where are they?

Natural causes come into consideration, too. A 1998 study of old cypress trees from Roanoke Island done by archaeologists indicates that after White left the colonists, the Roanoke area had its worst drought during a growing season in 800 years. The scramble for food might have pitted natives and colonists against each other, though it still wouldn't explain their total disappearance.

In 2009 Fred Willard wrote a lengthy research paper after examining the previously lost writings of Thomas Harriot, a naturalist who accompanied John White in 1585. Willard also investigated writings by earlier historians and studied early maps and drawings, including some by John White. And he discovered old deeds in courthouse records showing English surnames for some natives. Willard wrote, "The hypothesis for this paper is that the 1587 colony of Sir Walter Raleigh resettled 50 miles from their original settlement on Roanoke Island." Willard agrees with others that Raleigh sponsored the Roanoke voyages as a money-making project. But he suggests that it was more than precious metals that attracted the expeditions. Old abstracts refer to "secret commodities and a secret location." As a result of his research, Willard believes that the colonists had gone, as agreed earlier, to the secret location fifty miles inland where the commodities were silk worms and sassafras. The ability to produce silk would be profitable. Sassafras was used at the time to treat syphilis. Such resources could've earned Raleigh and others invested in the colony great wealth. If the colonists did make such a move, it's plausible that over time they were assimilated into the native community, and with subsequent English trips to the area, somebody must have known.

With ongoing archaeological exploration and DNA research, the mystery of the Lost Colony may eventually be solved. Then what?

A line in "The Story at The Lost Colony Genealogy and DNA Research Group" says if the truth about the Lost Colony is discovered, it would have "the much less interesting name of 'The Found Colonists.'" How would that play out as an outdoor drama?

CHAPTER TWO

Historic Gold Hill

In a warm North Carolina summer day in Gold Hill, North Carolina historian Vivian Pennington-Hopkins was sitting in an Amish glider outside Mauney's 1840 Store—a structure she'd saved from the bulldozer in 1990, which had since become a museum, shop, and tourist attraction. She felt somebody sit down beside her and move the seat back. She looked over to say hello but nobody was there. When she touched the seat next to her, it was much too chilly for the warm summer day. Vivian didn't say it was a ghost, but she did assert that what happened had no normal explanation. It's part of local lore but probably not old enough a story yet to be considered a Gold Hill legend. In this once booming gold rush town, now a small village dedicated to historic preservation and tourism, unexplained events are the stuff of daily life.

Gold rush? North Carolina? Didn't the gold rush start in California?

Nope. The first discoveries and their subsequent mining activity started in 1779 in the gently rolling clay of the central

Piedmont. A kid made the first find. Conrad, the twelve-year-old son of the German immigrant farmer John Reed, found a big, shiny rock in the Little Meadow Creek in an area near Charlotte. The rock weighed sixteen pounds, a lot of weight for a little boy, but he lugged it home. The Reeds didn't think much about it because they were busy cultivating the dense clay soil, which, though fertile, is hard to work. Moreover, this was not sixteen pounds of solid gold, just a rock with shiny streaks in it. John did take it to a silversmith in the nearby community of Concord, but all the silversmith knew was that the thing wasn't silver. So for several more years, the rock stood as a doorstop at the Reed home, until someone persuaded John to cart it off to Fayetville, more than one hundred miles away, for a jeweler's inspection. The jeweler knew what he had. He crushed the stone and melted out the mineral to make a gold bar, which Reed agreed to sell to him for the equivalent of about a week's wages—an amount measured in single-digit dollars. Later, he found out the jeweler was negotiating similar numbers for the bar, but with lots of added zeros, in the thousands of dollars. Somehow, John Reed managed to collect a fairer sum. Beginning to grasp the value of the odd rocks in their area, Reed and other farmers started wading through their streams looking for more gold-streaked rocks and, often enough, found them. The chase was on. Not that anybody gave up farming right away, but after a harvest, farmers would dig in their fields and streams looking for gold.

A geologist identified a vein of quartz streaked with gold that ran from Reed's place to Gold Hill, where gold was found at Andrew Troutman's farm in 1824. Before long, farmers and speculators were scrutinizing creek beds and digging in open areas, and they were finding a lot of gold. In time, the Gold Hill Mining District had twenty-three gold mines, with two of the most profitable in the area that is now the Gold Hill Mines Historic Park, a place created by local citizens for people to eat and play and remember. The Civil War and the discovery of gold in California spelled the end of North Carolina's gold rush, but back in the day, looking for gold progressed through placer mining, which is just digging in the dirt along the creek and panning for nuggets, to rockers. They were large screened devices that made it possible to sift more soil faster. Next came vein mining, digging quartz with gold in it from trenches. Then it was tunneling, sinking shafts deep into the land, excavating tunnels, and hauling out gold-streaked quartz. However it was acquired, the quartz then had to be ground and heated to melt out the gold. All the work was strenuous, but the mines were downright dangerous.

It must have been about then that the stories about spirits that never left began to form. Ghosts or specters or apparitions don't seem to come out of easy times, and life for the mining folks in Gold Hill was not easy. It was lively, though. The town became the center for mining activities in the area, with a population of almost three thousand people in the mid-1800s.

The Gold Hill Post Office was a center of communication for
the town during its gold rush days.

According to Vivian Pennington-Hopkins, the town had a post
office, several general stores, two doctors, a blacksmith, a hotel,
a wagon maker, and a shoe cobbler. At one point it also had
several brothels and a slew of saloons, so some of the apparitions
at the time might have come from spirits all right, but not those
of another world. Although some wealthy people were coming
to the area, or were getting wealthy shortly after arrival, life for
most folks involved with mining was hard. They lived in small,
uninsulated wood structures that were little more than shacks.
Many were immigrants who had known better conditions in

England, seduced by the possibility of getting rich from gold in America. Gold found in England would've belonged to the king, no matter who found it. In America it was finders keepers.

The most famous specter in local lore comes out of that atmosphere in the early 1800s, from Reed Gold Mine where Conrad had found the first gold. William Mills, an immigrant from Western Europe, was living with his wife in a cold, windy cabin heated only by wood fire. He was working hard, hoping to get rich. She was mostly complaining, as the story goes, because she had no place to wear the nice clothes she had brought with her, she was uncomfortable, and she hated this life. She died, either from a fall or by his hand when he couldn't stand her continuous berating. Who can say? Desperate to get rid of her body without having to explain her death, he hauled it from their cabin, though a snowstorm, to dump her down a deep shaft at the Reed mine. When people finally realized they hadn't seen Eleanor Mills for a while, William first said she was bedridden with an illness, and then later that she'd gone to visit relatives in Charleston. Soon he began hearing her shriek that it was cold and dark down in that tunnel and to get her out. He took to drink, and then disappeared, maybe to prospect in Dahlonega, Georgia, another place where a man might get rich on gold. Sometime after that, people began claiming to hear a woman screaming, over and over, to be helped out of the shaft. Naturally, they avoided that place at night. Even though the mine is now a state historic site, most tourists who have heard the story still wouldn't want to camp overnight anywhere near the old shaft. Just walking through one of the old mine tunnels with a tour guide and lamp is plenty scary.

Many more stories come from the Gold Hill village, which makes sense since this, after all, was the center of mining activity in the region. Vivian collected ten stories told by the old-timers about unexplained happenings in Gold Hill in her book *Gold Hill Ghosts and Other Legends*. Each is associated with the primitive, hard lives of the early miners. "Disease and death was just an accepted way of life," Vivian wrote. A favorite story is about a woman, a man, and his dog. It's one of those tales that never quite goes away. The man was Aaron Klein, the son of a Pennsylvania rabbi. Aaron wanted to get rich in Gold Hill, but he had a tough time there because many of the other miners weren't used to being around Jewish people, and they picked on him. He did have the regular company of a puppy he found, though, and then things got even better when he met Elizabeth Moyle, a young woman from England. They fell in love, planning to be married on Christmas Eve. One particularly rough miner, Stanly "Big Stan" Cukla, went into a rage when he heard the news, because he'd had designs on Elizabeth himself. Shortly thereafter, when the miners went to work at the Randolph mine, they found Aaron's puppy, obviously killed deliberately, at the mine shaft. Worse, Aaron was never seen again. A strange light soon began appearing around the mine, seeming to follow people, accompanied by what sounded like a puppy's whine.

This unnerved Big Stan, who started talking about going some-place else to work. Then he just didn't come to work one day. The other miners probably would have assumed he'd left as he said he would, had they not found his body at the bottom of an eight-hundred-foot shaft, underneath a hand-operated eleva-tor. They weren't sure whether he died trying to get to the gold before they did or somehow had been done in by Aaron from the other side. Elizabeth never married, but she never left the com-munity, either. She was buried in the Gold Hill Cemetery. Some people say they've seen her apparition wandering along the wall at the historic park or roaming the woods and streets, looking for Aaron. If the story ended there, it would be sweet, though maybe no big deal. But sometime in the twenty-first century, Aaron started showing up too. With his puppy dog.

For instance, a young man and his dog appeared sound-lessly behind a couple of anglers at the Gold Hill Pond. Only one of them saw him. As that one turned to speak, his friend asked who he was talking to, whereupon the young man with his puppy vanished. The anglers speculated that it was the ghost of Aaron Klein. Another time, around midnight, a park care-taker driving his pickup to check on the pond area saw a young woman walking with a backpack on her shoulder. He stopped so she could get by on the narrow road, but she just moved past, not seeming to notice the truck at all. When the caretaker looked back, she was gone. A favorite local supposition is that this was Elizabeth, like Aaron, keeping an eye on Gold Hill. If anybody's seen them together, though, it hasn't been reported. The older stories change over time, as legends do, but the newer accounts of more recent events have invited a mixture of skepticism and belief. Somebody once said nobody believes in ghosts except the people who've seen or heard them. There's been enough seeing and hearing in Gold Hill to bring several paranormal investigative groups, a filmmaker for the Travel Channel, and television crews from nearby areas to see what's going on. They focus especially on activities at the Montgomery Store, Mauney's 1840 Store, and the old powder house, where many strange things are reported to have happened, some actually caught on audiotape or video, others only the stuff of words.

In the Montgomery Store, where Vivian established a shop, a museum, a bluegrass music center, and a studio in which tourists can be photographed wearing old-time costumes, some people hear whispers, stairways creaking, and the sound of footsteps upstairs. In several investigations, technicians placed microphones inside the store after it was closed at night, then went out to their van to listen. The recorders in the van picked up the sounds of whispering and once, some thought, a woman saying, "I'm here." One of the investigators saw shadows inside the building, while musicians who've been playing bluegrass there have sometimes claimed to see shadows on the walls that couldn't be accounted for by any objects in the room. Music-loving ghosts? Vivian has also talked about doors opening by themselves and a burnt-out lightbulb in the attic coming back on just when she needed light up there in an emergency, then going dead again.

Across the street, at Mauney's 1840 Store, where Vivian first experienced a chilly presence in the glider next to her, night-time visitors to the area have reported seeing an older nineteenth-century couple, the woman with her hair in a bun, the man wearing a dark coat, looking out the store window long after the shop was closed. Another time, after the store was closed, an employee of the restaurant across the street who was waiting for a ride saw a child looking out the door window. This sighting was accompanied by near-paralyzing pain in the man's legs, which brought him to a halt. As the pain passed, the child disappeared too.

But the most tantalizing of Vivian's stories is the Powder House Ghost. "We're not sure whose spirit haunts the powder house," she wrote. She attributes finding out about it at all to a 2006 visit from the *Legend Hunters* film crew and the North Carolina Paranormal Research Team. The powder house is something like a root cellar, dug into the side of a hill as a place to store dynamite and other explosives used in mining. According to a story that has been passed down from old-timers, two miners went into the cellar to get dynamite. One of them lit a kerosene lamp. The other smacked a wooden crate with his pick to open the box, setting off an explosion that forced the pick into his chest and wounded the other miner as well. Attracted by the explosion, rescuers came upon a gory scene. The miner who had been impaled by his pick was also severely burned and died, cursing, shortly after rescuers had moved both men to the porch of the Gold Hill Mining Office. The other miner, though crippled, survived to tell this story that has been passed down. When Vivian, the film crew, and the investigators went to the powder house and opened the door, one of the men made a joke, inviting any resident spirit to show itself, calling, "Come and get me." Although some of the folks on the scene had a sense of motion somewhere in the vicinity, no spirit loomed in the doorway. But, of course, all of the crew were busy taking pictures anyway—that's what photographers do. When they looked at the photos later, a blue haze showed up on the picture taken to show the jester, as well as on another photo, taken outside, that had a fuzzy white image in the center. In Vivian's interpretation, one can discern the head and upper body of a man in a v-neck shirt or jacket. Some people, though, just see a white blur.

This wasn't Vivian's first odd experience with a Gold Hill photograph. An earlier one happened as she was making copies from an old photo of the old Gold Hill Mining Office in preparation for the visit from the Travel Channel's *Legend Hunters.* The photo had once belonged to Col. C. R. Hayes, the last mining engineer to live and work at Gold Hill. When he retired as engineer and manager, he continued to live in the manager's quarters in the office, along with many dogs. As the first copy of the photo came out of the copier, Vivian saw that in it the building appears to be surrounded by horizontal streaks of smoke. The second copy emerged from the machine looking perfectly normal, just a copy of the original. What stunned Vivian was knowing that about a year after the photograph was taken, the mining office burned, killing Col. Hayes, and she was making her copies more than thirty years later. She has included the "smoky" image and the ordinary one, side by side, in her book. Anyone looking at this picture can easily see the distortion of the first copy. Vivian concluded the tale with a question: "Can a residual haunting attach itself to a material object?"

She has been careful to say that nothing going on in Gold Hill is necessarily a haunting, and she's pointed out that even wind can make an old frame structure "talk." Speaking as an historian, she's also said that unexplained things do happen and are documented. And acknowledging the full-fledged skeptics who pooh-pooh all such tales, wherever they originate, Vivian said, "That's the fun part of the speculation."

In the introduction to his book *Tar Heel Ghosts,* John Harden (1903–1985), a journalist as well as a storyteller, responding to an old notion that the source of ghostly experiences was little more than indigestion, wrote about the relationship that seems to grow up between people who study the unexplained stories and the stories themselves. His observation was based partly on his own experiences as he researched and interviewed and wrote: "After living with these Tar Heel ghosts for some time I am convinced there is more to a ghost than the overloading of digestive apparatus. Ghosts, even if created in the mind and preserved in legend, can become real and personal."

Vivian might agree. Speaking of spirits and presences, she said, "I had never thought about that aspect of life." Her first introduction to such possibilities was modest. The deceased grandmother with whom she'd long shared a bedroom came to her in a dream, crying because what was being done to the old family house was going to make it look horrible. Two weeks after the dream, an uncle called to report to Vivian's mother that the old place had been sold and all the furniture handed over to an auction company—*two weeks ago*. Not a big deal, perhaps, but one that made it comfortable for Vivian to work with the strange events that have happened in Gold Hill.

Here's the question. How would you behave if such things started happening around you?

CHAPTER THREE

Pee Dee A.D.

own Creek Indian Mound, near Mt. Gilead in the southern Piedmont region of North Carolina, is the only state
historic site in North Carolina dedicated specifically to Native
American life. In 1927 there was nothing much to see here
except an earthen mound, which the owner of the land, Lloyd
Daniel Frutchey, had been thinking of flattening for cotton
farming. However, since local folks talked about arrowheads and
other relics that came to the surface, he decided instead to donate
a couple of acres to the state of North Carolina for anthropologi-
cal study and preservation.

Joffre Lanning Coe was an undergraduate student in
anthropology at the University of North Carolina in the 1930s
when he first visited Town Creek Indian Mound. He began
directing archaeological work in 1937, and fifty years later he
published his account of activity at Town Creek, beginning with
the observation that this would not be a final report because so
much study still remains to be done.

What could possibly be so interesting about a deserted site once inhabited by native people that one man would devote fifty years to studying it and still declare the work not finished?

Research, excavation, and reconstruction have been going on since 1937, an unusual length of time for such study, and because of Coe's long-range plan, excavation here was never a matter of just digging up artifacts and taking them away, as was the habit in places where the goal was simply to salvage what could be found before something like a dam or road construction destroyed whatever was buried. At Town Creek, excavation proceeded painstakingly, with workers digging and sifting one ten-foot-square area at a time. Often an excavated area was covered again with whatever was found left in place. Coe's idea was to map the entire site, square by square, to preserve for later study. Consequently, as excavation goes on today, slowly because of financial constraints, it enhances the earlier research. And it seems that the more archaeologists learn, the more new questions arise.

Sometime between A.D. 1100 and A.D. 1400, a group now known as Pee Dee natives settled here, establishing a community that seems to have thrived. Pee Dee is a cultural term, not a tribe name. The Pee Dee way of life was not unique to this area. It was part of what is known today as Mississippian society, which spread across southeastern North America beginning at about A.D. 1000. While their political and social cultures may have differed, these people, including the Pee Dee population, had in common using maize (a large-kernel variety of corn) and other cultivated crops for food, creating permanent towns, trading with other tribes, and building their public buildings on mounds, often within stockades. This would have been a gradual shift from the Woodland Period, about 1000 B.C. to A.D. 1100, when indigenous people still gathered wild food but had begun planting some garden crops, including tobacco, as well as making clay pots and hunting with bows and arrows rather than spears. As archaeologists and anthropologists learned about these other communities, it helped them understand Town Creek. But it also left many questions.

What attracted these natives to the Town Creek area? Could they have found it by following rivers? Town Creek is on the Little River. Little River flows into the Pee Dee River, which runs through northeastern South Carolina and into the Atlantic Ocean. Moving north, those early natives might have come to the same conclusion reached by many later settlers as well as contemporary North Carolina "transplants": Here is a great place to live. Even today the Town Creek area seems ideal for agriculture, hunting, and fishing. It is just a little higher than the flood plain, with great expanses of relatively flat, fertile land and dense pine forests. Access to rivers and creeks is easy.

The Pee Dee natives were not the first people to have lived at the Town Creek site. Archaeological excavation has found that the first mound was built over a collapsed, rectangular earth lodge that had been created by piling earth around its walls and on its roof. When the lodge collapsed, it was mounded with earth to create the base for a temple or town house. After that structure burned, more soil was put over it, creating a higher mound, upon which a new temple building replaced the burned one.

But whoever preceded them, the Pee Dees were apparently the largest and most highly organized community. They thrived for approximately two to three hundred years. Historic Site Manager Rich Thompson said researchers estimate that somewhere between three hundred and a thousand people may have lived within the stockade at one time. What happened to them? Where did they go? And why?

Reconstruction at the site includes a stockade and guard tower, a major ceremonial building on a mound, two temples, and a burial hut. The discoveries of ongoing excavation provide interpretations of how these structures were used, and give visitors a glimpse of Pee Dee culture as it developed sometime in the eleventh century A.D., which probably was the most active time in the site's history. Research may eventually find clues to what happened to the people later.

In his book *The Archaeology of Town Creek,* Edmond A. Boudreaux speculates that the move of native cultures like the Town Creek Pee Dees from earth lodges to public structures built on earthen mounds signaled a shift to a political system in which power came from rank and status rather than individual accomplishment. Or to put it another way, maybe your family background carried more influence than your hunting skill.

Thompson said there are probably more than five hundred burial sites within the Town Creek stockade, and excavation has revealed a lot about the kind of society in which the Pee Dees lived. Some people were buried in pits in a loosely flexed position, knees pointing out, but others were buried with fully extended limbs. Some people were buried with a variety of copper and shell artifacts, probably the result of trade, and suggesting high status in the society. Other sites revealed skeletons on their sides, with knees drawn toward the chin. In one, a large sherd lay on top of the body. Infants have been found buried in large urns apparently constructed specifically for funerals. Another grave contained the bones of five skeletons that seemed to have been buried elsewhere and moved later. Researchers hope that ongoing investigation will suggest more about the significance of the differing burials.

While many graves have been recovered with contents in place, bones from most of the first one hundred fifty were moved to the University of North Carolina/Chapel Hill to be studied. Examining such bones revealed another aspect of rank and status: how well the individuals ate. Elizabeth Monahan Driscoll, a graduate student in anthropology at the University of North Carolina/Chapel Hill, explained what scientists known as bioarchaeologists can learn in working with archaeologists to understand life at Town Creek. She wrote that by studying bones and teeth, bioarchaeologists can determine the approximate age of a subject, as well as gender and health. It seems that well before the days of high fructose corn syrup, too much corn in the diet could cause problems because of its high sugar content: dental cavities show up in the skeletal teeth. A diet made up of mostly corn and without much meat or fish for protein can cause anemia, which also shows up in bones. So do a host of other diseases, ranging from obvious ones like arthritis and osteoporosis to syphilis and tuberculosis. Driscoll wrote that research so far indicates an elite and a lower class. The upper class seems to have had better food and, correspondingly, better health.

Rich Thompson identified other questions about the Pee Dee people that may be harder to answer: "What was mundane, day-to-day life like? What were their routines? What did they do in their spare time? What made them laugh?" And then he asked a natural question for anyone who has been around children: "How did they occupy little children when it rained—kids without video?"

Some information can be inferred from a combination of bone study and what we know about how our own bodies react to our environment. For example, Carol Fantilli did a facial reconstruction from bones excavated in 1941 of a female about eighteen to twenty-five years old when she died. The woman had a face narrowing toward the chin, and she was short, about five feet tall. The reconstructed face has smooth brown skin, but Thompson said that in life it probably would've been blemished from living in an unventilated shelter with a pine fire. "We know that smoke would be hard on your skin," he said.

Based on the results of excavation combined with knowledge of other Mississippian native groups, archaeologists believe that in addition to being a place to live, Town Creek Indian Mound was a center for religious ceremonies, meetings, funerals, and burials. Systematic mapping and photography, with each section fitted into place, formed a sort of map, like an X-ray picture of the site. Today at the visitor center you can see dark spots of various shapes on a large map. The people who work at the center can point to an area and tell you what is below the surface there. For instance, Thompson identified established storage pits and a passage running to the river that probably was used to dump garbage. Before you get too appalled by the idea of dumping into a river, remember that in those days people didn't have the manufactured products that can trash a river or even a landfill today. No plastic bottles. No used batteries. No empty soup cans. No disposable diapers. Most garbage, perhaps all, that had to be discarded would have deteriorated naturally.

Mapping and excavation have also shown that as many as five stockades were built and destroyed around this area, only one of which has been reconstructed. Although we tend to think of stockades as protection from outside warriors, Thompson said their purpose was more likely to keep bears and wild animals out and little kids in. He said the routines of daily life were so demanding, he doubted there would have been a lot of war. "I just don't think they had time for that sort of thing."

Certainly ceremonies and rituals would have taken time. During the "busk," a period of physical cleansing, spiritual revitalization, and social renewal, a sort of new beginning, the natives would've cleaned everything in the area and repaired anything that needed it. In a biodegradable environment there would be lots to repair or replace. Ceremonial rituals with people from other villages would have taken time, too. Think about a family wedding or funeral or holiday celebration. Things wouldn't have moved any faster for the Pee Dees, and since nobody was flying in or parking the Honda in the driveway for a quick drive home, people probably stayed for days at a time.

The routines of keeping everybody in the community fed and clothed must have occupied much of the Pee Dees' time, too. If the Pee Dees wanted to make a simple meal of corn, greens, and squirrel meat, they would have had to catch and kill the squirrels and clean them, then roast or simmer the meat over a fire that they would have had to build from wood that needed to be cut first. Maybe the corn would be shelled and ground into a meal. Someone would have had to gather the greens and cook them, too. Then, in addition to fishing, hunting, growing, gathering, and preparing food, the Pee Dees needed some clothing. That would mean saving and curing animal skins and sewing them together. Weapons and tools had to be made. Ask a modern-day flint knapper how long it takes to make a single point.

The Pee Dees were making cooking utensils and other pottery, too, some of it quite sophisticated. Between the site's first exploration in 1937 and 1982, more than 500,000 pottery fragments were found at Town Creek. This brought another question to investigators. Designs on pots became more elaborate over time. Some were decorated by string-wrapped paddles that were pressed against the damp clay to make designs. Later the potters used wooden stamps to pattern the clay. As the pottery became more advanced, the number of burials here declined. Why? People didn't stop dying. Were they moving away or being buried elsewhere for some reason?

Excavation shows that the Pee Dee culture disappeared from this spot. Although some people apparently still lived here, they probably weren't Pee Dees. What makes an entire group of people move on? Researchers have suggested several possibilities. One is that something may have disrupted agriculture, perhaps an ongoing drought. "If you are completely dependent on what you can produce where you live for food, you could get very hungry very fast if crops fail," Thompson said. Even in recent years, periodic extended droughts have affected the Piedmont area of North Carolina. Or perhaps the population grew beyond the capacity of the land to supply food. Corn is a notoriously greedy feeder, and if the Pee Dees hadn't worked out ways to fertilize and replenish the soil, their crop yields may have become insufficient to feed the population. "If that happens, you've got to go somewhere," Thompson said. Another possibility is that the society may have broken down, scattering the natives. A contemporary example of such a phenomenon sometimes happens among Amish communities when they disagree on such issues as how much modernization to allow. Then they often split into several groups, each moving to a new location to start over, each with a somewhat different set of rules.

Whatever happened, the ongoing fascination this place holds for visitors, researchers, and volunteers is remarkable. So was the enthusiasm for the earliest work when research first began. Until 1960, the place was so undeveloped drinking water had to be hauled in for workers. The whole effort began during the Great Depression, so part of the work crew was from the Works Progress Administration (WPA), the "make-work program" for people without jobs. Housing was primitive. But the work went on and the reconstructions proceeded too. Nobody was getting rich here. Many residents in nearby Mt. Gilead invested time and energy in the project. Today, the state pays only a few people to work at the Town Creek National Historic Site, but they host visitors, especially classes of schoolchildren, with visible enthusiasm. The kids always have lots of questions, but new questions continue to arise, too. On June 24, 2009, Archie Smith, a former site director who became a volunteer, unearthed a clovis point, an artifact of such age it could mean the area was populated at least 3,000 years earlier. But not necessarily, Rich Thompson said, reflecting on other ways it could have come to Town Creek. It was found in a zone that once had been plowed, so who left it? Maybe a kid picked it up somewhere else as his family migrated and dropped it later. Or maybe it was part

A few ceremonial buildings at Town Creek Indian Mound and a stockade have been reconstructed at a site where archaeological remains are still being discovered and analyzed.

of an elder's collection. So far, there's no way to be sure of its significance at this site. In the preface to his book, published in 1995, Joffre Coe made an observation that could mean he saw such questions coming.

> The way into the past is devious and contains hidden pitfalls to entrap the unwary. The most that can be expected is a glimpse of the major landmarks shrouded in the fog of uncertainty as we pass back through the corridors of time. As people lived on the land, they inevitably altered its appearance. The inhabitants made things and lost them. They collected what they needed, and they discarded their refuse.

So today, as the questions continue, so does the research and the work of maintaining the place, much of it similar to the earliest days, repairing and replacing what is worn, and hosting ceremonies for people who come to learn about and celebrate Native American traditions.

CHAPTER FOUR

Tsul 'Kalu and the Judaculla Rock

High on the Blue Ridge Parkway in the North Carolina Mountains, at nearly 5,800 feet, massive rock outcroppings dominate the view. For those willing to climb a little, following the Devil's Courthouse Trail, a short trail paved by the North Carolina Park Service, one can see four states. A sign at the beginning of this trail reads,

THE BARE ROCK PROFILE NAMED DEVIL'S COURTHOUSE IS SINISTER IN APPEARANCE AND LEGEND.

Its "devilish" look has contributed to many folktales surrounding this mountain.

According to legend, a cave high on the mountain is the home of the Cherokee devil Tsul 'Kalu, anglicized in pronunciation to "Judaculla." Here he lives, dances, and holds court, ruling the Balsam Mountain range. At the base of the mountain, the Judaculla Rock site, near Cullowhee, in western North Carolina, combines a mystery with a legend. The soapstone rock is big, nearly two hundred square feet, and it's covered with etchings that nobody can interpret. According to Cherokee legend, the slant-eyed giant, Tsul 'Kalu, was Lord of the Hunt, a fierce, frightening creature with seven-fingered, handlike talons, who could leap from one mountain to another and became enraged if Cherokees encroached on his mountain hunting grounds and lair. Once, Cherokee hunters looking for game got into his territory. As he chased them, leaping from mountain to mountain, he landed on the rock. The etchings are the marks made by his nails. That's the legend. But the marks are clearly intentional. Who made them? Why? What do they mean?

And what about the legend's depiction of Tsul 'Kalu as a giant too ugly to behold? People who study such legends say they have some relationship to the lives of the people who have passed them down, a way to interpret events otherwise beyond their understanding. In Cherokee stories, Lord of the Hunt Tsul 'Kalu's arrows were lightning bolts; he could drink up a stream in a swallow; and his voice was a roar. That description would have helped early Cherokees explain drought, thunder, lightning, and bad luck in hunting. But what about his size and horrible appearance? Is he the Cherokee representation of the mythical monsters inherent in many cultures? Could Tsul 'Kalu be the Cherokee Sasquatch or Bigfoot, sort of a generic giant? Could it be that, no matter how sophisticated we become, we need big bad creatures to personify our fears and hopes? And maybe we need some proof that even the bad guys have a good side. The ongoing appearance of Tsul 'Kalu in Cartoon Network's show

The Secret Saturdays suggests that possibility. Perhaps it's hard being the ugly creature, too, no matter how powerful.

For example, in one old Cherokee story, a widow in the town of Kanuga, on the Pigeon River, had a daughter who was old enough to marry, but the mother insisted she not take a husband until she found a man who was a good hunter and would provide plenty of meat. Well, it took awhile. (Good men have always been hard to find.) But eventually someone showed up at their home after dark and declared his intentions. When he assured the girl that he was a fine hunter, she let him in to spend the night. Before first light, though, he said he had to go home, but that he'd left a deer outside for her mother. He came again the next night and in the morning left two deer. And then Mother wished he would leave some wood. He did, but sometimes men just don't get things right. He left whole uprooted trees, branches and all. Mother complained that he hadn't cut them up and stacked the wood, so the next night he made the trees disappear, leaving nothing at all there in the morning. Still, the romance continued, with the Great Hunter again bringing the girl game each night. Eventually the mother insisted she wanted to see her daughter's "husband." He said he didn't want to be seen because his appearance would scare her mother, but the girl persisted and finally the giant consented, warning her that her mother must not call him frightful. He kept his word and allowed himself to be seen the next morning. When the mother looked into her daughter's room and saw Tsul 'Kalu lying on the floor, she became hysterical. He was ugly, slanty-eyed, and so big he filled the room from top to bottom, which, predictably, sent the mother away screaming about how ugly he was. He went, maybe enraged, maybe with hurt feelings. But the story spins on, with the giant still coming back, and then asking his "wife" about a child. There is no child, the girl told him, just menstrual blood that her mother threw into the river. So Tsul 'Kalu went to the river, found a worm, and carried it back grown into a baby girl.

The giant persuaded the girl to escape this mother who hated him and tried to drown their child. So the giant and the girl took the baby and headed to the giant's home, Tsunegun'yi, where they had a second child. Meanwhile, the girl's brother, worried about his mother's loneliness, tracked down his sister by following the Tsul 'Kalu's big footprints. He found signs of a child walking along and, later, of another having been born. Eventually the brother came to the mountain upon which his sister lived with the Great Hunter and their children. His sister came down to meet him, but he never saw Tsul 'Kalu.

After four years, his sister showed up at her mother's house to say that her husband had been hunting in the woods nearby, and her mother and brother could see him if they came to the woods early in the morning. Even in legend you can't count on relatives showing up when they're supposed to. They didn't get there in time to see the family, but they found enough deer left hanging to feed the whole village.

The brother persisted in his attempts to see Tsul 'Kalu, and after frequent negotiation, the giant said the tribe could see him if they fasted in the townhouse at the bottom of the mountain for seven days, without coming out and without making a war cry. They followed the rules, except for one person from another tribe who sneaked out every night to eat. On the seventh day, thunderous noise from the mountain came closer and closer to the townhouse, frightening everyone into total silence except for the outsider, who was so scared he raced outside whooping war cries. The roaring stopped for a moment, then began again, fading into the distance. Even after this, the brother kept trying to see Tsul 'Kalu, but the giant declared no one would ever see him. It's a lot like a TV serial, this story, with promises, betrayals, reconciliations—all the classic stuff of the struggle between what we wish for and what actually happens, and the complications of trying to stay connected to those who matter. Did the story grow over time as Cherokees coped with their relationships and life events? Was the telling also a form of entertainment? And what about that rock?

Might the legend and the rock have another connection beyond "talon" marks? Could the engravings have anything to do with recording native legends, perhaps even in pre-Cherokee times? The one thing archaeologists agree upon is that the marks are intentional, not random etchings caused by erosion or weather. Technically, rocks carved like this are called petroglyphs or rock engravings, and there are at least fifty of them in North

The Judaculla Rock continues to mystify visitors and researchers alike with markings that nobody can interpret.

Carolina, though there are many more in the Western states. That's because the dryness there preserves them while atmospheric moisture in the Southeast tends to wear away the markings. Petroglyphs exist all over the world and usually date back to prehistoric times. They are not the same as pictographs or rock paintings, which are images painted *onto* rocks, while petroglyphs are pecked *into* the stone. Some of them contain recognizable figures—fanciful, almost-human beings, a caravan of sheep, fish, fowl, etc. Often there are also wavy lines and shapes that look like hands. Some analysts consider the figures a kind of notation used before the development of writing. However, the etchings on the Judaculla Rock, while clearly intentional, don't portray recognizable figures. Looking at them is a little like hearing a foreign language in a movie with captions—you *almost* understand the meaning. Archaeologists estimate the Judaculla engravings to be between two thousand and three thousand years old, but they can't use carbon dating for more accuracy because in times past people have used paint and chalk to make the markings more discernable, which makes the dating process impossible.

There may be more such rocks on the same property. Indigenous people quarried soapstone in the area to make utensils, and at least one other rock has come to light in modern times, but it was lost in a mining operation. Because this is a sacred place for Cherokees, no excavation to search for more engraved rocks or other artifacts has ever taken place and probably never will.

In the meantime, theories about the rock multiply, even as the markings become less pronounced because of weather, silt, and human interference. Could the engravings be a collection of religious symbols, as petroglyphs in some other places are believed to be, perhaps visualizations of a spirit world? Is this rock intended as a key to decoding some new language? What language, though, and who would have been speaking it? Maybe it's a map showing how to get from towns to the west and the Balsam Mountains to the east, since native people tended to travel in small family groups, but it's hard to imagine all those apparently random markings guiding travelers from one place to another. Another suggestion is that the rock depicts the Battle of Taliwa, which took place between the Cherokee and Creeks in 1755, although that doesn't fit with the estimated age of the engravings. Some people conjecture that it's a peace treaty, others, conversely, a battle plan.

The commonalities found in petroglyphs all over the world, including at Cullowhee, have led some scientists to postulate that the markings reflect an inherent, genetic aspect of the way human brains work. No proof, though.

The League of Energy Materialization and Unexplained phenomena Research (L.E.M.U.R.) is a team formed in 1994 that investigates the paranormal using scientific methods. After an investigation in August 2002, L.E.M.U.R. concluded that the markings on the Judaculla rock were made by an advanced culture, either from an earlier time on Earth or from another planet, to send a message to humans when they became sophisticated enough to understand it. The team said the marks are depictions of microscopic life that can be seen only with a microscope. However, Anton Van Leeuwenhoek didn't invent the microscope until 1674, and the rock's been around a lot longer. If you're not a believer in paranormal events, this notion is tough to accept, but the L.E.M.U.R. site (http://shadowboxent.brinkster .net/lemurhome.html) displays a large selection of images comparing photographs of microscopic life with markings on the Judaculla rock, including amoeba, diatom, hydra, trypanosome, and brucei worm. The similarities between the etchings and the photographs are striking.

At the other end of the theoretical spectrum, some observers think the markings are just doodles. Possibly, natives taking a break from the hunt amused themselves as they rested or passing time by pecking designs into the soapstone. Or maybe it was native kids. The rock is in a large, flat, grassy space that would have been a fine place for children to play while their mothers went about daily tasks, in which case the markings might be nothing more than the product of childhood imaginations.

Older children have had their turn at this place more recently. Students from Western Carolina University have gathered here in the dark of night for initiation ceremonies. They've reported spooky happenings: ghostly noises (whatever they sound like), a strange glow around the stone, and of course, UFOs in the grassy clearing. But it wouldn't be a proper initiation if it didn't seem scary.

Many people who have visited this site say the only way to form an opinion is to see it for yourself. The family on whose property the rock stands has donated it to Jackson County, and directions for getting there are public. Follow Business Route 23 through Sylva, go 1.3 miles to NC 107, turn left, and drive 8 miles. Then turn left onto Caney Fork Road, which is County Road 1737. Go 2.5 miles more, then make a left onto a gravel road and go 0.45 mile. You will find the rock on the right with a parking area on the left. The place has no facilities except for a viewing platform, which is intended to keep people from getting too close to the rock and adding their own inscriptions or otherwise damaging it. The county, historians, and scientists have expressed urgency about taking care of this artifact, preventing further desecration, erosion, and unintended damage. Advancing scientific technology may make it possible to learn much more about the rock. A sign asks visitors not to touch it or allow their dogs or children near it. We know what dogs would do. It might be about the same with children.

CHAPTER FIVE

The Sad Tale of Tom Dula

Sometimes a national legend gets all kinds of facts wrong, and the fiction just keeps on growing as the story gets passed down from generation to generation. The story of Tom Dula (pronounced Dooley) is a good example.

After two trials, Tom Dula was hanged on the first of May 1868 in Iredell County for the murder of his fiancé, Laura Foster, in Wilkes County. Laura's cousin, Ann Foster Melton, who had faced trial as an accomplice, was acquitted in a separate trial in the fall of 1868, probably because of a note dated April 30 that Dula had written shortly before his execution claiming sole responsibility for Laura's murder.

In the years since the murder, the tale of Tom Dula, his girlfriend Ann Foster Melton, and Ann's cousin Laura has become more and more romantic. The ballad about what happened, "Hang Down Your Head, Tom Dooley," written by Thomas Land shortly after Dula's death, was recorded by several groups, but it was the Kingston Trio's version, recorded in 1958, that spread the story's fame. That release sold more than six million copies, spreading the Dula legend not only across the nation but also into foreign countries as a crime of passion.

In recent times, the story has been dramatized every year in Wilkes County by the Wilkes Playmakers, in summer performances of the play *Tom Dula: A Wilkes County Resident,* written and directed by Karen Wheeling Reynolds. The players have put on the show every year since 2000. Publicity for the play says, "Folklore and legend feel that he confessed to the murder to protect his true love, Anne [sic] Melton." The event is really a celebration, with local musicians singing and playing acoustical instruments.

Karen Wheeling Reynolds, who has published a novel as well as her play about the events, said the story became famous in the United States at the time of the murder because North Carolina newspapers as well as *The New York Herald* covered Dula's two trials and his hanging extensively and dramatically. "This was before we had Jerry Springer and Oprah," Wheeling Reynolds said, "so it was a big deal."

The North Carolina novelist Sharyn McCrumb, who also has written often about events in western North Carolina, has called Tom Dula's story the first love-triangle murder to become national news.

Today, if you ask folks in Wilkes County, where the old stories have never died, many of them will say, "Ann did it."

And in 2001, one hundred fifty years after his death, citizens of Wilkes County signed a petition to exonerate Dula of the charges for which he'd been hanged. The pardon was circulated by the local newspaper, *The Record of Wilkes*. It languished on the desk of North Carolina Governor Mike Easley and never was approved officially. Karen Wheeling Reynolds said it's not clear why the petition never passed, but it probably wouldn't matter to Tom Dula anymore, and it gave the Dula legend a huge new boost. Reynolds said, "I will tell you the pardon request hit the Associated Press wire and we had info on all major news stations and in major newspapers across the U.S. Paul Harvey commented on it on his radio show. A crawler went across the CNN news saying 'Kingston Trio, where are you? They want to pardon Tom Dooley!' There are a lot of people out there that still remember Tom Dooley."

As the stories pass from one generation to another, Laura was beautiful, Tom was charming, and Ann married Melton only after Tom had gone off to fight for the Confederacy because she didn't believe he'd ever make it back alive. When Tom returned, the legend says, he became engaged to marry Laura, Ann's cousin. But the passion between Ann and Tom was so strong that they took up as lovers again, disregarding her marriage and his betrothal as well as Laura's rumored pregnancy.

Good stuff for a romantic legend. But what really happened? A few facts are certain: Ann was already married to James Melton when Tom left for the war; Laura Foster was murdered, then buried in a shallow grave; Tom Dula was hanged for it; and Ann Melton was found not guilty. But there's always been a good bit of popular

In the absence of any photos or portraits of Tom Dula made during his lifetime, the artist Edith F. Carter painted this portrait, depicting a young man handsome enough to charm the ladies.

sympathy for Tom, either as a besotted lover or a dupe. Was he really guilty? If not, who was? Why was Laura murdered in the first place? And if you strip away the romance of folklore, what were all these people really like?

By all accounts, Tom and Ann began their physical involvement as young teenagers and continued it even after Ann's marriage, apparently with her husband James's awareness. Tom Dula was supposed to have been handy with a fiddle and a banjo and entertained in Zebulon Vance's 26th North Carolina unit. Only he wasn't in that unit and, according to some reports, didn't play anything but a military drum. He was said to be handsome, about five feet nine inches tall, with dark curly hair and brown eyes. Nobody has any pictures that are definitely of him, but judging from his appeal to women, he probably was at least cute. He had a reputation for liking the girls and being able to engage them sexually. Military records show that he was a brave soldier, if not a hero.

Ann Foster Melton's background isn't so romantic either. She was one of Lotty Foster's five illegitimate children, promiscuous and illiterate like her mother, but in describing Ann at the time of Dula's execution, the *Herald* reporter wrote that she seemed poised and beautiful. Karen Wheeling Reynolds speculated that Ann may not have been especially beautiful but would have seemed so compared to many local girls because Melton, a shoemaker who owned his farm, was not poor like most of the characters in this drama. "There was food, and there was money," Reynolds said. "That would have made it possible for Ann to dress nicely and make a good appearance. A true trophy wife." However, she clearly was not monogamous, and many statements from her court trial claimed she often bedded down with Tom while her husband, James Melton, slept in another bed in the same room.

Laura Foster, Ann's cousin, had four younger siblings, raised by her father, Wilson Foster, a poor tenant farmer, after her mother died. She still lived at home. Court testimony indicates that she, too, was sexually active beginning in her early teens, though in the many years following her murder, local folks defended her as sweet and kind, sometimes commenting that she was frail. ("Frail," however, was a term sometimes used in the area to suggest loose morals.) In local lore, Laura was pregnant, but if so, why wasn't that mentioned in her autopsy report?

Laura disappeared on May 25, 1866. Early that morning, she'd talked to Tom at her bedroom window. When he left, she got dressed and, taking her father's horse, followed a path along the Yadkin River, where she met a friend whom she told she was going to meet Tom at the Bates place, an abandoned and overgrown blacksmith shop, to elope. After that, nobody saw her alive except whoever killed her. At first, nobody thought much of her absence. Her father, William Foster, is supposed to have said he didn't care where she was, he just wanted his horse back. In time, the horse came home with a frayed rope halter. But by early summer, local people had begun looking for Laura, starting at the Bates place, where they found a ragged rope that matched the one on the horse, tied to a dogwood tree. One man who helped during the search testified at the trial that Tom Dula never joined in the hunt.

Gossip began spreading the notion that Tom had something to do with Laura's disappearance and might be arrested, which led him to run off to Tennessee, change his last name to Hall, and take work on the farm of James Grayson to earn money for new boots.

There was still no sign of Laura or her body, but a justice of the peace put out a warrant for Dula's arrest, and two deputies from Wilkes County went to Grayson's farm to get him. It's not clear how they knew where he was. At any rate, apparently he'd learned they were coming because he had just left. So, taking Grayson along, the deputies caught up with Tom near Mountain City. He didn't put up a fight and was taken back to Wilkesboro and jailed.

When you've got a man in jail for murder, it's a good idea to figure out what happened to the victim. Perline (Pauline in some stories) Foster, Ann Foster Melton's cousin, who worked in the Melton home, got the hunt started when she was heard telling people she knew where Laura was buried. That led the authorities to pick her up as a suspect. Perline said Ann had come to her crying because she was afraid Tom would be hanged, and she wanted to show Perline where Laura was buried. Perline led authorities to the general area but refused to go all the way, and by September searchers on horseback were combing the woods. Following Perline's directions, the searchers found a blood spot along the road; a little less than a mile beyond that, they found Laura's grave. This was probably about the first of September 1866, some time after the earlier searches. Nobody had noticed the grave before because loose soil had been removed and the spot re-covered with sod so that nothing looked disturbed. It was a horse's reaction to a blood spot on the ground nearby that led searchers to look more closely. They found Laura's body in this shallow grave, lying legs bent, on her side, face up, covered with an extra dress she'd apparently been carrying as she ran away. The coroner who examined the body at the site said she had been stabbed between the third and fourth ribs. He did not mention pregnancy. Now Perline Foster was no longer a suspect, but based on Perline's statements, Ann Foster Melton was. She was arrested and confined in a cell on the other side of a solid wall next to the one where Tom was incarcerated.

The bill of indictment for their trial accused Tom of murdering Laura, and Ann of getting him to do it, then harboring him afterward. The prosecutor dropped the last part and accused her only of influencing Tom to commit the murder. The lawyer Zebulon Vance (later to become governor of North Carolina) came forward to defend Tom and Ann pro bono, not because Tom was in his military unit, as some storytellers have said, but possibly because he wasn't real busy right then, and the defense would be good publicity for his political future. The first thing he did was insist that neither Tom nor Ann could get a fair trial in Wilkes County, where local opinions about them ran strong. The venue was changed to Statesville, the Iredell County seat, with a notably insecure jail from which several prisoners had escaped. The next thing Vance did was move that Tom and Ann be tried separately lest anything either of them said in self-defense be used against the other. This motion was granted.

For almost two years, Ann remained in jail as Tom was tried. She never testified but was sometimes in the courtroom listening to the proceedings. A jury found Tom guilty. He was sentenced to death. But Vance managed to get a new trial after some pretty nitpicky objections from his defense. For example: "2nd Objection to Bill of Indictment. It is not specified in the body of the bill that the offense is alleged to have been committed in the State of North Carolina." The people who testified during the trial often told different stories or had differing views of what they'd seen and heard. It was a little like the old game where players sit in a circle and whisper a beginning message to the next player, until the messages comes back to where it began.

The fun of that game is how wildly different the returning message is from the one in the beginning, something like going from "my arm itches" to "I farm in britches." But this wasn't fun. Some of the testimony involved different stories about the actions of Tom, Ann, Laura, and Perline in the time before Laura's murder, much of it sordid. To put it simply, there was a lot of sex, coming and going, crying, and disease. Perline said the day before Laura disappeared, Tom had borrowed a mattock from Ann's parents, to widen a path in the woods, he claimed, and Ann got a canteen of whiskey, maybe so he could get Laura drunk. Ann and Tom left the Meltons' and were gone all night, then Ann showed up in wet clothing in the morning, went to bed, and slept most of the day.

This doesn't make it into the legends, but court records say that Laura, Tom, Ann, Perline, and James Melton all had syphilis, and revenge on Laura for passing it on to Tom was suggested as a strong motive for murder. Some local talk also suggested that Perline also had been with Tom and loved him, murdered Laura, then skillfully set up Ann to get them both out of the way. If so, things didn't quite go as she'd planned. Another version is that she wanted to get back at Tom for passing syphilis on to her. In that case, everything may have worked out exactly as she intended. At any rate, Tom was convicted and never got out of jail, though he came close to escaping shortly before his execution.

John Foster West researched the story extensively, studying court records, trial data, and military accounts. Because his own family had lived in the area where the events happened, he understood the hard life of this part of the South during Reconstruction after the Civil War, when food was scarce, work was hard, and education was sometimes minimal. In his book *The Ballad of Tom Dula,* published in the 1970s, West tried to give a dispassionate account of what was known about the case. In 1993 he published a revised version of the story, *Lift Up Your Head, Tom Dooley,* based on even more research. His personal conclusion was not about Dula's guilt or innocence. Instead, he said Dula simply did not have a fair trial. First, Dula was arrested by North Carolina deputies in the state of Tennessee, outside their jurisdiction, without a proper warrant for that state. Also, the evidence against him in trial was entirely circumstantial. And not only were statements of testimony contradictory, dates on court papers differed wildly in documenting arrest and court actions. Whether anybody's paying attention to this would have made any difference at the time we don't know, but it might in a more modern court.

After all avenues of appeal were gone, Tom Dula remained perky in his jail cell, joking and refusing spiritual counsel until right before his execution day, when a jailer discovered that, using a piece of glass, Tom had nearly cut his way through the leg chain that chained him to the wall. Once free of the shackle, he could have escaped the jail, as had previous inmates. Finally, when he saw that his execution was inevitable, he wrote (or had written) with a pencil this note:

Statement of Thomas C. Dula – I declare that I am the only person that had any hand in the murder of Laura Foster

April 30, 1868

As was the custom in the area, Dula rode a horse-drawn wagon to the town square where he was executed, not to a white oak tree in a lonesome valley as the ballad would have it. In one truly preposterous story that has circulated, he sat on his coffin on the wagon, playing a banjo on the way to his hanging, and joked when he saw the noose that if he'd known it was going to be such nice clean rope, he'd have washed his neck. In fact, he spent the ride assuring his sister that he had made his peace with God. So Tom Dula was hanged after riding on his own coffin atop a wagon, all right, but as he stood with a noose around his neck, he wasn't joking. He spoke to the huge assembled crowd at length about politics, the Confederacy, dishonest testimony against him, and his spiritual redemption. Then he threw the crowd a ringer. The *Herald* newspaper article quotes his final words: "Gentlemen, do you see this hand? I never harmed a hair on Laura Foster's head." Of course the hanging went on anyway.

If he didn't kill Laura, who did? We'll probably never know if Ann did it in a fit of jealous rage because she didn't want Tom to marry Laura or because she blamed Laura for giving syphilis to Tom, who in turn infected her, or if Perline wielded the knife. Or was the culprit someone else entirely? Even Tom Dula's final note raises questions. It was written "crudely" with a pencil, but Tom was supposed to be illiterate and had signed earlier documents with an X. During his two years in jail, might he have learned at least rudimentary writing skills, or did someone write that note for him? If so, who? And why?

After nearly two years in jail, Ann Melton was tried shortly after Dula's death as an accomplice in the murder but was quickly acquitted, probably because of that final note. The *Herald* reporter wrote that she had the poise and grace of a fine lady. After two years in jail, could that have been true?

Ann must have had some kind of remarkable charm because after her trial ended, her husband, James Melton, came to take her home and playwright Karen Wheeling Reynolds said the couple had two children. But in the mid-1870s, Ann reportedly died a terrible death, deranged from the syphilis, seeing visions of hell, and some say she confessed to a part in the murder.

Somehow, though, the known facts and the speculation don't override the legend of the country's first love triangle crime of passion. As the legend persists, so does the triangle. Laura Foster is buried near Highway 268 close to Ferguson in Wilkes County. Tom Dula is buried by Highway 11134, now known as Tom Dula Road, across the Yadkin River from Ferguson. Ann Melton is buried near Highway 1159. Tourists who follow the Tom Dula Trail from site to site move in an approximate triangle through romantically scenic rural country. As Karen Wheeling Reynolds said, "The whole story isn't pretty, but the legend is."

CHAPTER 6

Blackbeard the Pirate

Blackbeard often is called North Carolina's most notorious pirate. These days, he is arguably North Carolina's most popular pirate, too, what with his role in movies and museums and poems and even electronic games. The trouble is you get a different notion of him from every source you consider. What did he look like? Nobody knows, except that he was tall and bearded. What was his real name? Although he's commonly referred to as Edward Teach or Edward Thatch, he may have made up those names. Some historians say he was really Edward Drummond. Was he fiercely ruthless or pretty decent as pirates go? Did he really have fourteen wives? Did he bury treasure before he died or spend all his loot on good times? Nobody has certain answers. This much we do know for sure: He was killed in a bloody battle on a British sloop that the commander, Lieutenant Robert Maynard, tricked him into boarding with some of his pirate crew on November 22, 1718. After he fell, the surviving British sailors cut off his head and hung it from the bowsprit of their ship to prove he was dead so that Maynard could collect a £100 bounty put out on Blackbeard by the governor of Virginia. Whatever happened to that head? As recently as the twentieth century, several people claimed to have seen the skull, and one man looking for it offers a reward of $1,000 to the person who can produce it.

What's the real story behind all the romantic yarns? Even serious biographers can't get a full handle on the conflicting tales of Blackbeard's life, partly because the original sources they consult, letters from those involved at the time and newspaper accounts of his activities, are only as accurate as their authors, and official documents are hard to find. Modern-day scholars have the additional challenge of filtering their research through their own personal perceptions. For instance, in 1960, Hugh F. Rankin, from the department of history at Tulane University, wrote for the North Carolina State Department of Archives and History in *The Pirates of Colonial North Carolina* that Blackbeard was a "piece of human trash." On the other hand, Robert E. Lee, dean and professor of law emeritus at Wake Forest University, wrote in *Blackbeard the Pirate: A Reappraisal of His Life and Times,* first published in 1974, that it is a common error to judge historical figures by the moral standards of the present. "Piracy for a long time was a way of life for the adventuresome. There was at first no really strong public sentiment to suppress it." Also, some early writers weren't above adding fictional, lurid details to their work to make a good story.

In any case, Blackbeard was actually a pirate for only two years, from 1716 to 1718, a remarkably short time in which to build the reputation that continues into modern day. He was probably a sailor much earlier though, serving as a commissioned privateer on a British ship during the War of the Spanish Succession, also known as Queen Anne's War, which lasted from 1701 to 1713. In that capacity it would have been legal for him to plunder Spanish ships for the British Crown. After Britain stopped fighting that war in 1713, which would have left Blackbeard unemployed, he simply continued his activities, becoming a pirate, gathering booty for himself rather than any government. He started out on the crew of Captain Benjamin Hornigold, and after that crew overthrew Hornigold, Blackbeard became captain of one of his ships, *La Concorde,* which once had been a French slave ship. When he took over as captain, Blackbeard renamed the ship *Queen Anne's Revenge* and armed her heavily, presumably for more aggressive piracy.

When he plundered other ships, what did he take? By all accounts, everything he could, from food to weapons and whatever else might have value in trade. Whether such piracy involved bloody fights and murder or just the power of intimidation depends on whose story you believe. Early writings are full of tales about walking the plank, tossing victims overboard, and occasionally shooting a crew member just to maintain authority. But current interpretations increasingly hold that Blackbeard, and many other pirates, worked hard to appear ferocious and intimidate people so they wouldn't have to do battle and actually kill anyone. At least not unnecessarily.

There's no way today to know for sure. Certainly Blackbeard dressed for intimidation. His biographers had never actually seen him, he never had a portrait painted, and old letters vary in what they say about his appearance, but descriptions of his attire consistently tell us that he draped his body with pistols, knives, and swords and somehow wore lit hemp fuses around his face before threatening a fight. It's not clear whether he wove the burning cords into his long beard, braided them into his hair, or tucked them under his tricornered hat. Having a tall, heavily armed pirate coming toward you with smoking hair and a fierce reputation might be plenty enough to encourage docile surrender of whatever a ship was carrying, especially since the sailors didn't own the goods and weren't very well paid for their work.

Although North Carolina claims Blackbeard as her pirate, he sailed, plundered, and traded up and down the Atlantic Coast, especially earning fame for his blockade of Charleston, South Carolina, in May 1718, the same year he was killed. With his flagship, *Queen Anne's Revenge,* and three sloops, he cornered five merchant ships at Charleston Harbor and kept any others from using the harbor. He captured about eighty of Charleston's leading citizens, who had been aboard one of the ships, and held them hostage until the city met his demands. Interestingly, it wasn't money Blackbeard wanted but medical supplies. Given the lives of sailors and also places they'd spent time—the West

Indies and Central America—speculation has been that some of the crew needed treatment for venereal disease or yellow fever. In any case, when Blackbeard's emissaries finally returned to the ship after several days, the hostages were released, but only after the crew took most of their clothes.

A little later, *Queen Anne's Revenge* ran aground at Topsail Inlet, near what is now the town of Beaufort, as did his smaller ship, *Adventure. Revenge* was too damaged to sail. Many biographers believe this was part of Blackbeard's scheme to cut down the size of his crews, which had grown to number about three hundred. Blackbeard and a small group of his favorite men left in a smaller sloop, stranding the rest of the crew. Historians conjecture that Blackbeard's plan was to set up headquarters and a trading site in the area. He was apparently on good terms with North Carolina Governor Charles Eden and could have expected no problems with such a plan. Indeed, the governor pardoned him, and a pardon from England also was on the way for all who gave up piracy. In *Blackbeard the Pirate*, Robert E. Lee asserts that Blackbeard was married by Governor Eden in Bath to a girl about sixteen years old. In all probability the other thirteen or so wives attributed to Blackbeard were of the girl-in-every-port variety or inventions of writers making a story more exciting. Anyhow, it seems that for a time, the pirate may have settled into calmer life with Mrs. Teach at Bath. Did he run short of funds or just get restless, or was he following preset plans all along? We'll probably never know. In any event, he was soon back in the

EDWARD TEACH

B 47

Notorious pirate called "Blackbeard." Lived in Bath while Charles Eden was governor. Killed at Ocracoke. 1718.

Jon C. Lakey

Blackbeard wasn't the type to settle down, but Bath may be the closest he had to a hometown.

trade. The North Carolina coast was close enough to Virginia to make Virginia Governor Alexander Spotswood uneasy about Blackbeard's proximity. To get rid of him, Spotswood commissioned two small sloops as British ships (remember, Virginia was still a British colony) and put Lieutenant Robert Maynard in command of fifty-six men aboard *Ranger* and *Jane* to eliminate the Blackbeard threat.

The confrontation occurred in the inlet after a day of maneuvering and a night of waiting. Some of Maynard's men on *Jane* were killed; the rest pursued *Adventure* and then hid below deck, luring Blackbeard and a few men into boarding. By all accounts Teach fought violently, even after having been shot and stabbed over and over again. According to newspaper stories of the time, Maynard decapitated the pirate after he died, and the men threw the rest of the body overboard. After he was thrown overboard, the story goes, the headless Blackbeard swam around the ship three times, or maybe seven, before sinking from view.

The victorious British sailors hung Blackbeard's head from a pole extending from the bowsprit of their ship as a warning to all other pirates to stay away, and some accounts say it remained in place as the sloop sailed to the colony of Virginia to collect the bounty. But since that head was worth 100 pounds in Virginia, the crew soon may have put it away in a safer place until getting there.

And then what? Assuming the victorious British sailors took the head ashore to collect the bounty, what happened to it next? A common explanation is that the head hung from a pole on a riverbank near Newport News, Virginia, in an area now known as "Blackbeard's Point," warning off all would-be pirates, and eventually ended up as the base of a silver-plated punch bowl called "the infant." Angus Konstam, author of *Blackbeard,* claims to have seen the artifact at the Mariner's Museum in Newport News. In 1930 a respected North Carolina judge, Charles Harry Whedbee, wrote a story about drinking from the skull as part of a secret fraternal ritual on Ocracoke Island. Whedbee insisted the skull never left Ocracoke. Even earlier, though, one John

Watson wrote that the head was used as a drinking bowl at the Raleigh Tavern in Williamsburg, Virginia. Good stories all. Whedbee was either a great storyteller or a true believer because he offered a reward of $1,000 to anyone who could bring the cup to him to X-ray for authenticity. He must have been pretty convincing because writer and pirate buff John Walker grew interested in the story. When he tried to get in touch with the judge, he learned that Whedbee had died just weeks earlier. Still, Walker persisted. He contacted not only Whedbee's publishers but also those of other authors who had written about Blackbeard, as well as museums, traveling many miles looking for information about the head. As part of his quest, recounted in his own words on the Internet (www.ocracoke-nc.com /blackbeard/treasure/blackbeards-skull.shtml), Walker offers a reward of $1,000 for information giving him the opportunity to examine the skull and determine its authenticity. Walker's quest led him to track down leads that information about the skull, or the skull itself, might be somewhere in Bath, at the University of Virginia, at William and Mary College, somewhere in England, or in the hands of a private collector in New England. Meanwhile, other folks, knowing what outdoor elements can do to bones in a relatively short time, say the skull probably just deteriorated as it hung by the river.

Well, what about the treasure, then? Was there any? While Blackbeard was reputed to have buried treasure in various areas of the North Carolina coast, nobody has ever reported finding any, and not for want of trying. Given his reputation for high living when he was on land, he could well have spent it all. Indeed, considering his ongoing popularity in tourism, fiction, film, and theater, he may have earned more after his death than he did when he was a-pirating. And if you believe one popular legend, he may yet get to enjoy it. Every so often someone claims to see an apparition of Blackbeard looking for his head. What would happen if he found it and it was plated with silver?

This story doesn't have a real ending yet. Each new biographer has found, or claimed to have found, reasons to question earlier information. As recently as 2008, Kevin P. Duffus, author of *The Last Days of Black Beard the Pirate,* wrote that Blackbeard wasn't Teach or Thatch or Drummond at all, that he was quite possibly Edward, the son of James Beard, who died before the baby's birth. In the Duffus version, "Black" would have been a nickname used as we sometimes find a "Red" or "Brownie" or "Shortie." Thus, "Black Beard." Having set forth that claim, Duffus refers to "Black Beard" throughout the rest of his book. In fact, he says that his research proves almost everything we've ever read or heard about the pirate's wicked behavior was based on early sensational fabrication that, over time, came to be accepted as documented fact.

We may come closer to some provable truths in the ongoing excavation of the ship found in 1996 in the inlet, now known as Bath Inlet, where *Queen Anne's Revenge* is acknowledged to have run aground. The research is slow, painstaking, short on funds, but ongoing. The people working on the project are convinced that they've found *Revenge,* although that hasn't been proved definitely. A detailed, year-by-year account of what paid and volunteer workers are finding and analyzing at www .qaronline.org makes it clear that they believe they're studying the remains of *Revenge.* And if you're looking for adventure, they need volunteers.

CHAPTER SEVEN

Brown Mountain Lights

I t was a dark night. Now, this wasn't a first date, but they were still in the early stages of getting to know each other, and when he suggested stopping at the overlook on Morganton Road, near Linville Falls, to check out the Brown Mountain Lights, she wondered if he was pulling a new version of driving to a secluded parking spot to "watch the submarine races."

"No, seriously," he said, "stories about mysterious Brown Mountain lights go way back to the Cherokees."

Aside from the possible stars in her eyes at some point, are there really any lights to be seen from Brown Mountain? And are the stories actually old, or are they just hype to attract tourists?

Tales of the lights do, indeed, date back many generations, and while there is mention of seeing the lights in Cherokee stories, they didn't quite become legends. Some early settlers did believe the lights were the spirits of native Catawba and Cherokee warriors who died in mountain battles. And in a Cherokee version, the lights were the spirits of Indian women looking for their men who'd been killed fighting.

In a Southern story, a slave set out to search for a planter from the Low Country who got lost while hunting in the mountains. The slave, carrying a lantern, roamed the mountains looking for his master, but eventually left or died, leaving behind his spirit with a lantern that still shines.

Then there's the story of a woman who disappeared in about 1850. People of the community believed her husband had killed her, and they took to the mountain looking for her or for her body. When they saw lights on Brown Mountain, they decided that was her spirit haunting her husband while telling the searchers not to look for her anymore. She never came back nor did they ever find her body, though many years later someone discovered skeletal bones that some folks decided were those of the woman who'd disappeared.

The descriptions of the lights vary as much as the stories about spirits that cause them. Variously the lights have been said to look like balls of fire, white bobbling blips, hovering reddish lights, fast moving, and stationary. Sometimes they seem to drift and fade, at other times to spin and shoot away. None of these behaviors fits another old notion that the lights come from a parade of military ghosts doomed to march back and forth across the mountain forever carrying candles.

These days, some people believe that all the stories are hokum because not everybody who looks sees lights. Still, some of the descriptions reportedly based on observation support the claim that there's something to see—at least sometimes.

A story published in the September 23, 1924, *Charlotte Observer* described the ". . . mysterious light that is seen just above the horizon almost every night from Rattlesnake Knob, near Cold Spring, on the Morganton road" as unexplained. Whoever wrote the article was either a good storyteller or a good reporter. Consider this description: "With punctual regularity the light rises in a southeasterly direction from the point of observation just over the lower slope of Brown Mountain, first about 7:30 p.m., again about 20 or 30 minutes later and again at 10 o'clock. It looks much like a toy fire balloon, a distinct ball, with no 'atmosphere' about it, and as nearly as the average observer can measure it, about the size of a toy balloon."

Contrast that with the somewhat miffed reports from an Appalachian State University research team posted on the Internet on March 15, 2005: "We continue to make trips to this viewing site but remain frustrated at not seeing the lights. Our general feeling is that the lights seen by most people most of the time are ordinary lights such as campfires, campers' flashlights, car head and tail lights, lights of planes taking off from the Morganton-Lenoir Airport."

The problem with that interpretation is twofold. Recorded sightings date well before motorized vehicles with lights existed, and campfires tend to stay on the ground where you start them, not go bobbing off into the atmosphere.

A similar objection arises in response to a scientific investigation made by the U.S. Geological Survey in 1913. Researchers decided the lights were from locomotives in the valley, but reports of the sightings didn't stop when a massive flood washed away roads and railroad bridges there.

A German engineer, Gerard William de Brahm, saw the lights in 1771 and attributed them to burning nitrous vapors in the wind that caught fire and then burned out when they bumped into each other.

For all their skepticism, or perhaps in the interest of scientific objectivity, researchers at Appalachian State University have maintained a comprehensive listing of earlier references about the lights at www.brownmountainlights.org. In a particularly detailed report from the second U.S. Geological Survey, published in 1922, now available on this Appalachian State website, the author, George Rogers Mansfield, who did see unexplained lights, summarized and mostly discounted all theories available at the time. He also spent many hours observing the dark skies, testing rocks and soil of the surroundings, and interviewing both local people and visitors, concluding that the phenomenon was interesting but unexplained.

Some of the natural causes to which the lights have been attributed include swamp gas, phosphorus, radium ore, and fire or signal lights from moonshine stills. But rays from radium are invisible, phosphorous does not occur in a free state, and swamp gas forms in marshy areas, which aren't part of this area's

CRAIG DISTL

This overlook just outside Morganton is maintained as a spot
from which one might view the Brown Mountain Lights at night,
if and when they appear.

geology. As for stills, surely they weren't there before white
men got to the mountains, nor do that many survive today. In
another suggestion reported by Mansfield, Mr. H. C. Martin
speculated that the lights are mirages caused by air currents of
different temperatures and density coming together. But here
Mansfield seems a bit testy when he faults that idea: "A mirage
is a phenomenon of the daytime rather than of the night."

That brings up another complication: Reports differ on
when it's possible to see the Brown Mountain Lights and from
where. The mountain is in the Pisgah National Forest of the

Blue Ridge Mountains. Popular places from which to watch for lights include Brown Mountain Overlook, twenty miles north of Morganton on NC Highway 181; Wiseman's View Overlook, five miles south of Linville Falls on State Road 1238; and Lost Cove Cliffs Overlook on the Blue Ridge Parkway at mile post 310. Some people report that as the trees have grown taller below the overlooks it's difficult to see into the space below, but Morganton's mayor, Mel Cohen, took steps to correct that. He entered into a joint effort with city, county, and state officials to cut back the growth at the overlook and clean up the place. The U.S. Forest Service cut nearly 200 trees, with further cooperation in refurbishing the site coming from the Burk County Tourism Development Authority and the North Carolina Department of Transportation, as well as some local programs.

No matter where you go to watch, it has to be after dark, presumably on clear nights with no moonlight, but some people have seen the lights when it was hazy and sprinkling. The best times are supposed to be about 10:00 p.m. and 2:00 a.m., especially in September and October, the locals say. And the lights appear, when they do, not against the mountain but in the atmosphere above it. The tourism people admit sightings are "a somewhat rare occurrence," which differs from old reports of their being frequent. This brings up yet another question: Could it be that whatever has caused the lights is somehow diminishing in force?

Or does it say something about the patience of would-be observers with demands on their time and lots of electronic toys for more comfortable diversions at home? Perhaps one must be singled-minded and undistracted to see anything. One off-duty park ranger who went to a Blue Ridge Parkway overlook to watch for the lights said he never saw any. "But," he admitted, "beer was involved."

The Appalachian State researchers operate with minimal funds and much other work to do, so they can't camp out waiting to see something. They haven't found any particular time to be efficacious and suggest just going when it's convenient.

Speculation about the Brown Mountain Lights shows up in just about every book you can find on unusual occurrences in North Carolina, as well as on myriad Internet websites, oriented toward everything from the paranormal to Appalachian State's scientific research. Inevitably, when you look into unexplained phenomena, you can almost always find an extraterrestrial explanation. In her 1979 book *Southern Ghosts,* Nancy Roberts, one of the earliest and most prolific writers about strange and unexplained events in the South, introduces the UFO theory in a passage that deserves to be passed on in its entirety:

> But, perhaps, the most exciting explanation of all for the lights has been overlooked. In recent years the theory has been advanced that the mystery lights are UFOs and that this remote area is a gathering place for the flying saucers whose extra-terrestrial

beings use them to land and later take off after the visitors gather information about our planet.

"What irony if as we explore space seeking life on other planets, we are being observed and have been for centuries by the very beings we are attempting to contact through inter-planetary travel and radio communication.

How's that for a nighttime date—not submarine races, but UFO watches?

CHAPTER EIGHT

Apparition at Maco Station

Every kid should learn the word "apparition." *The Oxford English Dictionary* defines it as "A remarkable thing making a sudden appearance." So when an adult scoffs, "You're just seeing things," the young one can say, "Actually, it's an apparition." The big word wins. And since it's an apparition, something just might be there to see. Edward Howell, from the North Carolina paranormal investigation group NC Haints, Apparitions, Ghosts, and Spirits (NC HAGS), said, "My understanding of apparitions is that they are a sudden appearance of the unexpected. Now to most people, that would refer to the naked eye seeing this appearance. I think it may also be a sudden appearance that you see in a reflection or something caught by camera that you really were not expecting." NC HAGS, based in Raleigh, North Carolina, investigates sites where paranormal events have been reported. Their strategy is to document their experiences and findings and report them, leaving the matter of belief to each individual.

In North Carolina, people of all ages have been seeing things for a long time. One old story that NC HAGS checked into was that of Joe Baldwin at Maco Station. Joe was a dedicated railroad conductor working the Wilmington-Florence-Augusta line. In 1867 he was standing in the rear coach, his train heading home to Wilmington. As the train approached the little Maco Station, which had been known as Farmer's Turnout earlier, Joe felt it slowing down. He knew something had to be wrong because no stop was scheduled there. Then he realized that the coach had come uncoupled from the rest of the train and was slowing to a halt. A second train was roaring full speed toward Joe's train, and the engineer would have no way of realizing that he was approaching a stopped car on the track. According to some versions of the story, Joe raced along the coach urging passengers to jump out as he headed to the rear platform to warn the oncoming train of his loose car. He grabbed a signal lantern and waved it repeatedly from the platform, but the second train kept on coming. Joe waved the signal light until the moment the train slammed into the stopped car. In a huge crash, the coach was destroyed and Joe was decapitated. His lantern flew into the swamp by the tracks and his head landed somewhere else. In some accounts, a whole group of cars had separated from the main train, and Joe's frantic signaling came from the caboose. There's some disagreement, too, about where Joe's head went. In any case, nobody could find it and his body was buried headless. That's the legend.

Not long after the crash, people began saying they'd seen mysterious lights along the train tracks. Usually they reported a white light that looked like a swinging signal lantern moving up and down the tracks at Maco Station. It appeared so often that train engineers running this route started using red and green signal lights so their signals wouldn't be confused with the phantom white light. In October 1894, President Grover Cleveland said he saw the light from his Pullman. Or is the more accurate story that the year was 1889 and that when he left his presidential coach to stretch his legs at Maco Station, where the train stopped to take on water and fuel, he asked a signalman why their signal lights were red and green? In that case, he heard about the white light; he didn't see it.

Not only have versions of the story varied, but descriptions of the light's behavior have too. Once it was reported to have chased after a couple of kids and, on another occasion, scared a soldier home on leave. One time, it flew off in an arc and landed near the spot where the lantern was said to have fallen after the wreck. Sometimes it was bright and glowing, sometimes dim. On occasion it has moved toward an observer and then moved back. Old railroaders have said the light could fool them into stopping a train, then simply disappear. Popular lore had two explanations. Either Joe was looking for his head or Joe was still trying to warn oncoming trains of danger because he didn't know he was dead.

In his book *Tar Heel Ghosts,* published in 1954, Jim Harden wrote that watching the lights at Maco Station had become a popular jaunt for party groups who would park their cars nearby and walk toward the tracks in high good humor, then fall into silence as they reached the site. After the light appeared, the partiers would try to figure out what they'd just seen and somebody would inevitably tell the story of Joe Baldwin. Folks left in a subdued mood.

Then after the railroad tracks were torn up in 1977, and the trestle bridge over which they ran had fallen apart, it seemed the party was over. Hardly anyone reported seeing lights. But Eddie Howell and the rest of the NC HAGS team got to wondering about the old stories. "I knew people from way back that talked of seeing the light back in the day, especially Nancy Roberts and her book. We thought maybe something would still be there even though the tracks are gone."

The group made its first scouting trip February 10, 2007, during the day. They had a little trouble locating the spot where the accident had happened, and local people didn't seem to want to talk about it. But eventually they did find the spot, as well as a bit of track in the area. They went back for a full-scale investigation March 10, 2007, at night. Here's Eddie's account of the experience.

> When we went to where the Maco Light used to be seen near Wilmington, we knew what we were up against. The original tracks had been pulled up in 1977 and very few sightings of Joe Baldwin had been reported since that time. This did not deter us from trying to make contact with Joe. When I took four non-flash

camera pictures and asked him to show himself, I really did not expect anything to be on the frames. The camera did not have a view screen on the back, so I had to wait until the next day to upload them to the computer. To my amazement, in the third picture was a greenish outline of something. This turned out to be an odd outline of what we believe to be Joe Baldwin. The photo was analyzed later by a photographic expert and he showed us more in the picture than we previously had seen. In some way was this an apparition? It all depends on your definition of apparition.

The NC HAGS website, www.nchags.org, provides a link to YouTube videos of the group's investigation as well as the images captured by Eddie's camera. Whether the pictures show a silhouette is as much a matter of opinion as the definition of apparition, but added notations in one frame suggest which markings would represent the head, the decapitated body, and then the lantern some distance away. When you look at the picture that way, you can see the possibility. Another YouTube video accessible from the NC HAGS site shows a computerized simulation from a man in Pennsylvania re-creating his 1962 experience at Maco. Here the light looks the way the most frequent reports used to describe it—a bright ball moving down the track, seeming to get closer and closer, then backing up and disappearing.

Such unexplained lights, often called ghost lights or spook lights or earth lights, are not unique to North Carolina or even the United States. The Brown Mountain Lights come into this category too, although their described behavior differs from what's been reported at Maco. Often such lights are named according to where they've been seen—Chapel Hill Light and Cove City Light, for instance. Sometimes they get more jazzy names, like Devil's Racetrack Lights (near Diamond Grove, North Carolina). Aside from paranormal explanations, people offer several standard modern interpretations of such phenomena—headlights from a nearby vehicle, reflections from some other light in the area, or phosphorescent swamp gas especially. Generally, though, such explanations don't fit with what people say they've seen. At Maco, the lights were reported well before automobiles traveled a paved road anywhere nearby, and they moved in what appeared to be an intentional pattern, unlike reflections or swamp gas. So what are people seeing when they see ghost lights?

You have to wonder, too, what inspires a bunch of people, like the NC HAGS Paranormal Observers, who have "real" jobs and other interests, to devote time and energy to chasing down lights and apparitions and spooky unexplained events.

Eddie said he was originally motivated to start such investigations to help people who were encountering phenomena they didn't understand, as he had. He grew up in a haunted house where his parents wouldn't acknowledge or even talk about the events he was experiencing. "Nobody would believe me," he said. "I thought I was going crazy." As a teenager, he was

EDWARD HOWELL

Paranormal investigator Eddie Howell on railroad tracks near the abandoned
Maco Station site where he photographed an apparition.

reassured about his sanity one night when he and some friends
with whom he had a rock band were gathered in his basement
bedroom. "All of a sudden the door rattled and then it opened
by itself, and everybody ran out the back door."

Another reassuring influence was Nancy Roberts (1924–
2008), who wrote more than twenty books dealing with legends, mysteries, and ghosts, mainly but not exclusively in the
southeast. Eddie recalled, "She came and talked to us at our
elementary school many years ago. I have friends that remember
her fondly." (Her story about the light at Maco Station was one

impetus for his Maco Station visits.) As an adult, he's found other people with similar interests and a shared notion of how to pursue them. That's how the NC HAGS team came together. "We decided early on we didn't want to be famous and we didn't want to make a dime. We're trying to help people." They agreed, also, to use only first names in public statements. And each of them began the quest for reasons similar to Eddie's. He described Mike as "truly empathic" who sometimes will speak only one sentence during an investigation, a low-key, reliable person. Jeff is a skeptic. "He's interested but he wants it proved." Andy was "somewhat clairvoyant" as a child but lost the ability during his teenage years. Now he's trying to relearn it. The team has kept a low profile, except for their videos, which are NC HAGS's form of reporting. They never claim to have found the only answer to what they experience, but verify, when they can, that something beyond the norm seemed to be happening. Here again, many years later, Nancy Roberts's influence had an impact on Eddie. "She was gracious enough to let us use her picture for our video. She actually called me here at my house. I felt very honored."

Eddie said they are careful never to leave any inappropriate language in their video accounts, even if they were startled into an expletive at some point during recording, because they know children and families watch the videos. "We want to be good role models." He said this investigation team has had help from several other people with similar interests: the Heritage Hunters Society, Paranormal Scene Investigators, GHOSTS of

Raleigh, Sherrie James, and Scott Nicholson, though certainly not all at once. No parties. In fact, Eddie said his team's excursions are done quietly because if people knew about a trip, many would want to come along. "You'd have a busload everywhere you went." Those parties of the 1950s wouldn't work for serious research.

What would be your explanation for stories about the Maco lights? You probably can't test it at Maco Station anymore, because the site is on private property and nobody can go there without permission from the owner. That raises one more question, a little like whether or not a tree falling in the woods makes a sound if nobody is there to hear it. Does an apparition exist if nobody is around to see it?

CHAPTER NINE

The Devil's Tramping Ground

If you were to visit the Devil's Tramping Ground, near Siler City in Chatham County, you'd find that the mysteries and legends about this place are a lot more interesting than the site itself. What you'd find today is a more or less circular path in a remote wooded area, on private property, where nothing much grows. Not only is the path itself barren with only a little scrub grass inside the circle, but people who've tried to transplant this grass have said that it won't root anywhere else. As recently as the 1940s, the circle was reportedly about forty feet in diameter with a more dramatically obvious absence of growth.

According to old stories, the Devil's Tramping Ground felt so evil and frightening nobody could stay a night within the circle, dogs broke free of their leashes as they approached it, and anything left inside it would be moved out by morning. Cars stopped running if you drove too close. Even though the circle is smaller now and its lack of growth less pronounced than it was said to be for centuries, it still fascinates people. Some visit and believe; others come and leave scoffing.

Nobody has ever really explained the phenomenon of this dead zone. Most old legends associate the place with ancient evil, while contemporary scientific explanations leave unanswered questions, and other speculation introduces all sorts of oddities.

The oldest stories come from Cherokee legend. John Harden offers two in his book *The Devil's Tramping Ground and Other North Carolina Mystery Stories,* published by the University of North Carolina Press in 1949. One is that when Indian tribes met here for special occasions, the braves wore a circular path doing war dances appealing to the Great Spirit for victory in their battles. In this interpretation, the Spirit has prevented anything from growing here as an honor to those tribes. In another version, this is where Chief Croatan was killed in a battle with a rival Indian tribe, then later buried here, and the Great Spirit has kept the spot barren to honor the chief. That ties in with another of North Carolina's enduring mysteries—the Lost Colony of Roanoke). In this theory, the word "Croatoan" that the English sailors found when they returned to Roanoke with supplies to find the colony empty was believed to be a message that the colonists had gone to join what remained of the Croatan tribe after it moved to the eastern part of the state.

In the 1700s some early settlers in the area also attributed the phenomenon to indigenous tribes, figuring it was a spot where they'd held ceremonies that somehow killed the grass. Well, okay, but why did it stay dead over generations?

A later version was that the Great Spirit kept the area from making new growth as a permanent reminder of the way indigenous tribes were mistreated by colonists and Americans. The problem here is that some of the legends predated the arrival of colonists.

For a while, the notion that horses and mules harnessed to a molasses mill created the path as they walked round and round to power the mill held sway, but the idea lost credibility because at other treadmill locations, the vegetation returned after the operation ceased.

Some scientists have found that the soil in the circle is high in salt and was possibly once a salt lick for deer and other animals. Wouldn't all that licking have exhausted the salt supply over the centuries, and why would the salt have formed a circle to begin with?

How about the scientific assertion that the soil here is just too acidic and low in nutrients to support growth? In writing his book, John Harden had soil samples from the circle tested by the North Carolina Department of Agriculture, which reported that the soil was sterile. It was too acidic and low in nutrients. This seems like a good explanation until you try to account for the circle? Moreover, why would plants grow right up to the perimeter of the circle and stop?

Some other theories that have come along include the circle being a place for Druid meetings or a location where animals were sacrificed in satanic ceremonies. And, of course, occasionally one hears the inevitable UFO conjecture. By far the most enduring explanation, though, has been that the Devil does it while he's pacing around scheming new disasters for humans—hence the name, Devil's Tramping Ground. Current reactions to the place are as varied as the old tales. Where once we'd have read these in magazines and newspapers, these days they're more likely to show up on the Internet, on websites and blogs.

One account comes from Tom Chase, who writes for the astrology magazine *Welcome to Planet Earth*. He was educated in electrical engineering and computer science, so he certainly understands the physical laws of nature. But in a lengthy article copyrighted in 1997 (www.zodiacal.com/articles/chase/valujet .htm), Chase uses astrology and biblical symbolism to analyze the forces related to the 1996 crash of Valujet Plane 592 in Florida, drawing connections between the Devil's Tramping Ground and that crash. In part, he argues that the number of people who died on Flight 592 is 110 and the Tramping Ground is by Highway 1110. Chase suggests that astrology might explain other crashes, but it doesn't really explain the Tramping Ground.

In a more grounded story, Kady Harrington, writing for Haunted North Carolina Paranormal Research & Investigations (www.hauntednc.com/legends_dtg.htm) at the end of January 2010, recalled that although according to legend, the Devil would toss out any objects left inside his circle and boot out people who tried to sleep there, camping gear and all, she found trash within the circle. "Apparently Satan didn't mind a few beer bottles in his lair," she wrote.

The Tramping Ground has become a place for young males to test their courage, too, which might explain some litter as well as the campfire remains in the circle photographed by Dr. John Shillito, MD. Dr. Shillito said the Tramping Ground, as he found it in 2001, is not a very impressive site. "The most one can say for it is that it is a roughly circular area devoid of any vegetation in the midst of a woodsy section."

Some kids have reported indifference to being there, while others were seriously frightened. A brief account at Haunt Spot (www.hauntspot.com/haunt/usa/north-carolina/devils-stomping -ground.shtml) quotes a teenager who stood inside the circle with friends: "It felt like a large hand rose from the ground and grabbed my heart." He said it hurt so he couldn't move, and he couldn't get up from his knees until he apologized to the entity for trespassing. Trading blog messages, other teens have variously said that nothing much happened but they won't go back, or that being there made them uneasy in some vague way. One complained that on Halloween night in 2009, their fire wouldn't stay lit and they heard sounds that gave them a creepy feeling. How much of this can be explained by trespassing on private property at night, in a remote, dark, wooded area, possibly with underage beer drinking figuring into the experience?

It's not just kids who've had fairly recent experiences that unnerved them, though. In 2004 Bobette Bryan posted a story

This photo by Dr. John Shillito, MD, shows that the Devil's Tramping Ground
is not as startlingly circular and barren as it had been a few decades ago,
though nothing inside the circle grows vigorously.

for *Underworld Tales* magazine (www.underworldtales.com/devil
.htm) describing the experience of Ethan Feinsilven, a journalist, who had decided in October 1998 to debunk all the stories
about the Devil's Tramping Ground by spending the night in his
tent inside the circle with his two dogs. He did. But according
to Bryan's report, Feinsilven was uneasy, hearing "ghostly" footsteps, and left the next morning believing there was something
sinister about the site. Bryan, who claims she has investigated
hauntings extensively, says she thinks someone is buried there,
probably murdered, and doesn't want to be disturbed. Bobette
calls the reported happenings "a haunting" and suggested curious
people check out the spot themselves.

A woman writing under the name "Liv" (www.greensboring
.com) tried to do so on July 23, 2006. She loaded her four-year-
old son into the car and headed toward the site using a GPS
system and a map. As she followed ever-narrowing roads, she
took pictures of muddy paths and clear-cut woods areas. Light
rain turned into "buckets," and the closer she got to what she
thought was the Tramping Ground, the harder it rained. When
she thought she'd have to leave the car and walk to the circle,
she turned around instead and headed home. She told the story
jokingly but didn't deny feeling uneasy and glad to be heading
back out of Chatham County. Blog responses to her write-up
said she'd actually been in an area being cleared for development, not at the Tramping Ground. (Finding the place has been
somewhat confusing since the North Carolina Department of

Transportation named the scenic byway there Devil's *Stomping* Ground Road.) Such responses gave more specific directions to the Tramping Ground. It makes you wonder if just the *idea* of a haunted place is scary enough for most of us.

This leaves us with two mysteries, really. Perhaps a question even greater than what caused the circle in the beginning is why people remain fascinated by it and the stories about it even as its physical appearance dims. Dr. Jonathan Crane, who teaches communication studies at the University of North Carolina in Charlotte and is the author of a book on horror films, *Terror and Everyday Life: Singular Moments in the History of the Horror Film,* offered this suggestion: "Every state, region, and town in the country has its spooky hollows, houses, and haunts. Even though we 'know' that the devil and his minions are unlikely to hold residence in our neck of the woods, we maintain and cultivate these legends to preserve collective title to our state and our town. This land is our land, and one of the ways we keep title is to people our places with fantastic creatures of our own creation. If you live here, you know the stories. If you don't know the story, then you are a stranger. And anyone who has ever heard a legend, Jack-Tale, or ghost story knows how to regard strangers. Of course once you've been told the story, you are no longer a stranger."

You've learned the story. Now the big question: Given the opportunity, would you spend a night at the Devil's Tramping Ground?

CHAPTER TEN

The Ballad of Frankie Silver

Three days before Christmas in 1831, Frances Stewart Silver killed her husband, Charles, with an axe at their log cabin in mountainous Mitchell County. She cut up his body, tried to burn some of it, and buried some more at several different places in the area. On July 12, 1833, she was hanged for the crime. Frankie was about seventeen years old, Charlie about eighteen. Their daughter, Nancy, was just a year old. The story has been passed down, one generation to the next, ever since. The fact and dates of the murder and Frankie's hanging are verifiable. Almost everything else that happened is open to question.

Why would a young mother kill the husband she needed to help maintain the home, bring in food and firewood, and provide for their little girl? Why would she try to dispose of his body in such a gory way? Could she, in fact, have managed such a monumental task by herself?

The story that has grown up around the events and has been part of local lore told to generations of children at home and school pictures this as a crime of jealousy and revenge. Here's how the tale goes.

Charlie Silver was a lively, good-looking, strapping guy who could charm the girls and, like most mountain men, liked his whiskey. He and Frankie had a nice romance until sometime after their daughter, Nancy, was born; then, gradually, Frankie became more and more interested in Nancy and paid increasingly less attention to Charlie. So maybe a healthy young guy might stray a little bit—understandable, really. But whenever he was away from home any length of time, especially overnight, legend says, Frankie was wildly jealous and, over time, began plotting revenge for his supposed infidelities. Her chance came shortly before Christmas, when he came in from chopping wood, maybe after a nip or two, and lay down in front of the fireplace to play with his little girl. Shortly, he fell asleep with his head on a small stool padded by his coonskin cap, and Nancy went to sleep on his chest. Frankie moved the sleeping child to a bed, grabbed the axe by the fireplace, and gave her husband a fatal whack. Then she had to figure out what to do with his body.

At this point, some versions of the story say she got help from her mother, Barbara, and her younger brother, Blackstone, to chop up Charlie's body, burn some of it with his clothes in the fireplace, and haul the rest to several different sites to bury them.

However it transpired, that is what happened to Charlie's remains. It introduces another question: Where was little Nancy all the while?

Next morning, Frankie walked up to her in-laws' place and told them Charlie hadn't been home for two days and claimed that she wondered where he was. Later, she went back to tell them that she still hadn't seen him and didn't care if she never saw him again because she and Nancy were going to her parents' house. In contemporary accounts, several members of Frankie's family helped her with trying to hide all traces of Charlie, which took a couple of days, and then sent her off on that trip to tell Charlie's family she hadn't seen him.

But someone claimed to have seen Charlie headed toward his own house a day or so before he went missing. Moreover, in a light snow his foot tracks had headed toward his house while none had gone away from there. When he didn't show up anywhere in about a week, the Silver family started looking for him in earnest. They searched in the mountain woods and along the river in the icy cold winter weather. Eventually, they went to his house and, checking there, found pieces of bone among the ashes in the fireplace, then more bone outside in ashes near the spring, with signs that an entire winter's supply of firewood had been burned.

The legends gets fanciful here, with some stories saying searchers found Charlie's head in a hollow tree stump, others that it was his torso, and others that his dog, Drum, found his bloody coonskin cap and from that tracked some of his remains. However it happened, Frankie, her mother, and younger brother were arrested on January 10 and locked in the Morganton jail

Because Charlie Silver's body parts were found buried in several places and the family didn't want to dig them up, each spot is marked with a stone and another marker gives full details of his birth date and death.

for the murder, purely on circumstantial evidence. Since this was well before the days of DNA testing, we don't even know for sure how they decided that what they found was Charlie. Three days later, Frankie's father demanded a hearing before a magistrate on the grounds that there was no evidence against the three. Mother and brother were released for lack of evidence, but Frankie was kept in jail and ultimately indicted for murder.

In his book *Nancy's Story: To Right the Legend of Frankie Silver,* which tells the tale from the child's point of view, Jim Harbin wrote that Frankie's mother and brother may have been released because the evidence wasn't strong enough to hang all three of them and the sheriff said he'd rather score at least one conviction than none at all. Harbin took much of his information from a diary that Nancy Silver kept as an adult. How accurately would a child's experiences translate into the perceptions of an adult's diary?

In Nancy's version, Frankie killed Charlie in self-defense after he came in drunk and mean, with his rifle aimed at her, and possibly threatened the child as well. Frankie grabbed the axe and acted in desperation. When he was dead, not knowing what to do next, she ran to her parents for help and the whole family tried to help her eliminate the evidence, not realizing at first that she had acted in self-defense, which shouldn't have been considered criminal. In the view of Nancy's grandfather, Frankie's father, once they'd tried to hide Charlie's remains, self-defense seemed harder to demonstrate. Frankie's father, who was afraid that he and his wife and son, as well as Frankie, could all be hanged, urged Frankie not to tell anything about what had happened, saying, "Don't worry, they won't hang ya." Apparently, it was a fairly common, though erroneous, belief that no judge would hang a woman.

Frankie's trial opened March 29, 1832. The jury reported the next day that they were deadlocked nine to three in favor of acquittal and asked to hear from some of the witnesses again. After that, they unanimously found Frankie guilty. Judge Donnell sentenced her to hang and set the date for the coming July. Her lawyer asked for an appeal, which the judge filed with the North Carolina Supreme Court. No counsel appeared on her behalf. In June, that court denied the appeal and instructed Frankie's execution be held in the fall term of Burke Superior Court. Only there was no fall term because the Burke County judge was seriously injured in a fall, so it took until spring of 1833 for that court to set a new execution date—June 28.

These details and more are set out in a heavily researched account written by Perry Deane Young, *The Untold Story of Frankie Silver: Was She Unjustly Hanged?,* in an effort to debunk the myths and tell the story accurately. "The problem with history," he wrote, "is that too much of it is written too quickly and taken from stories and files that are themselves full of mistakes." Ferreting out accurate information produces a much more interesting story, he said.

Among facts Young verified are that Frankie escaped from jail with the help of her family on May 18, 1833, but was found, with her hair cut short like a boy's, and returned to jail along with her father and uncle and one other man who wasn't identified in available records.

As events were developing, and perhaps as the reality that Frankie really would hang sank in, some local feelings about her became sympathetic. Two petitions for her pardon were filed. The first, signed even by some men who'd been on the convicting jury, was submitted to North Carolina Governor Montfort Stokes. He rejected it. A year later, some locally influential women got involved. This second petition, printed in full in *Nancy's Story,* was drawn up by Nicholas Woodfin, a Buncombe County attorney, on behalf of the petitioning women and delivered to the new North Carolina governor, David L. Swain. The women argued that "the husband of the unfortunate Creature now before you . . ." was neither a good husband nor parent, leaving all work, including what should have been his responsibility, to his wife. The document says, "The neighborhood people are convinced that his treatment to her was both unbecoming and cruel very often and at the time too when female Delicacy would most forbid it. He treated her with personal violence."

This points back to the fact that because Frankie had pleaded "not guilty," no self-defense arguments could have been entered into evidence at her trial. Moreover, she did not testify in her own defense, possibly because her father said he didn't believe she'd be found guilty on such circumstantial evidence, much less sentenced to the gallows. (He may have feared anything she said could incriminate the rest of the family.)

Governor Swain wrote to the petitioners as though the hanging had already taken place so a pardon would be too late. Was he confused or pretending, as some contemporary accounts suggest, so as to avoid the matter? But with this much public support, why would Governor Swain refuse a pardon? Could power and money have been involved? Because the Silver family owned a lot of land, which meant they had influence, politicians in the area may have pressured the governor not to upset the Silvers by pardoning the woman who had been convicted of murdering their son. Governor Swain had granted Frankie a two-week delay before the execution for her to "prepare herself" for death. Now what was that all about? So why would he then have written that letter as if the execution had already happened?

She was hanged on July 12, 1833.

As study over time has shown, the stories about Frankie's execution day are mostly wrong, and some of them downright distasteful. Contrary to popular notion, Frankie Silver was not the first woman to be hanged in North Carolina. Nor was she the first white woman to be hanged—not even the first woman in Burke County. As for the actual event, she did not sing from the gallows a long ballad she'd written admitting her guilt. She didn't even write one. Some say "The Ballad of Frankie Silver," which exists now in several different versions running to fifteen stanzas, was written by a Methodist minister. It claims guilt:

> For month and days I spent my time
> Thinking how to commit this crime . . .

and urges others not to take a similar path.

On the gallows, the preacher may have invited Frankie to confess, but her father is said to have yelled, "Frankie, die with it in ye." Today some people believe that if he really did say that, he was not referring so much to her own guilt as to the involvement of any of the rest of her family in what had happened. Was he willing to sacrifice one daughter to protect the rest of the family, including himself? A wooden fence reportedly was built around the gallows, some have thought to allow the Silvers privacy from gawkers who might be on the scene, but Harbin contends that it was to keep the crowd from moving in to grab souvenirs of the event, apparently a custom at the time. And then there is the fanciful account of the cake she was supposed to have in her hand on the way to the gallows. An old "Ripley's Believe It or Not!" published July 13, 1833, says she refused to be hanged until she had finished "every last crumb" of the cake. If you were about to be hanged, would you care about cake? Since all this transpired in the days before radio, television, video cameras, and cell phones that can show events in progress, we'll never know exactly what happened.

And yet younger generations keep trying to move past the myths and grasp the realities. The extent of these efforts, going well beyond satisfying tourist curiosity, is as interesting as the legend that has inspired them.

At least two films telling Frankie's story have been produced, each introducing possible explanations for what happened and for why she wasn't granted clemency. One of the filmmakers, Theresa Phillips, actually reworked her first version of *The Ballad of Frankie Silver,* which she started filming in 1998, to create a new version, released in 2010, that she said will do a better job of reflecting her view of the story. Like many children growing up in the North Carolina mountains, Theresa had often heard the story as she was growing up. "It was the traditional story, that she was evil and did a terrible thing and so on, but it never rang true to me. And it always bothered me that we didn't hear what happened to the little girl, Nancy." Theresa met Perry Deane Young, generally considered one of the major researchers of Frankie's life, in Yancy County. They talked and he shared much of his research with her. Theresa's resulting film emphasized the story from Nancy's point of view, as does her 2010 version.

The Frankie story made it to the stage, too. Western Piedmont Community College sponsored a play, *They Won't Hang a Woman,* that was performed by a local cast. Another play, written by the sister-in-law of Senator Sam Ervin, was produced at the Repertory Theater at Mars Hill College. Drama teacher Howard Williams, a native of Morganton, wrote the play *The Legend of Frankie Silver,* which was produced at Brewton-Parker College in Georgia in 1993. A company from Switzerland presented the ballet *The Ballad of Frankie Silver* in

Atlanta, Georgia, during the 1996 Summer Olympics as part of the Cultural Olympiad.

The story has also been the stuff of lectures and books. The North Carolina Museum of History featured a special program with author and historian Maxine McCall making a presentation. (The audience was invited to bring a lunch.) Perhaps the best-known account of those long-ago events is Sharyn McCrumb's novel *The Ballad of Frankie Silver,* published in 1998. In this novel, she interweaves the story of a fictional trial and execution with her deeply researched account of what happened to Frankie Silver and her belief that things might have been different if the Stewarts, like the Silvers, had money and power, but they did not. Some teachers of English literature have used this novel to teach the relationship between factual account and fictional narrative, and how the two may be combined.

McCrumb is a descendant of one of Frankie Silver's brothers, a Stewart. That helps explain her involvement in the topic, but many people in the Silver family, which is very large, also continue their interest in the story. Some are writing or have written articles and stories of their own. Nor are these necessarily in defense of Charlie's behavior or to accuse Frankie. At a Silver family reunion in 1997, McCrumb read from the manuscript of her novel, just before its publication, which makes the case that Frankie was not fairly treated. Beverly Patterson, who was there, later presented a paper about Frankie and the family at a 1997 meeting of the American Folklore Society. It was also published in the *Journal of American Folklore*. Patterson said McCrumb's reading was the highlight of the Silver family reunion.

Patterson also described a fascinating continuation of the Frankie Silver story as people continue to try to figure it out as a schoolwide integrated unit. At the Heritage Middle School in Valdese, not far from Morganton, Jo Ball's eighth-grade English class staged a "retrial" of Frankie Silver. For several years all the eighth-grade faculty have used the Frankie unit to teach everything from North Carolina history and social studies to math and science. The trial is the final event of the project. In the "trial" that Patterson witnessed in 1997, the jury of eighth-graders and some parents, after hearing the testimony, acquitted Frankie for the fifth consecutive year. In these trials, Frankie testified in her own defense, which did not happen in her real 1832 trial. After one year's session, the eighth graders sent a petition for Frankie's posthumous pardon to the North Carolina Governor's office, where it received only passing attention from an assistant attorney general. The kids who know Frankie's story must wonder if anybody ever gives serious attention to petitions, present or past.

Why won't this story go away? Legends often settle into a comfortable "entertainment" category with only the occasional inquiry into historical facts. What is so compelling about Frankie Silver's story that people keep looking for truth about something that happened in 1831? How would events unfold if something similar happened today?

CHAPTER ELEVEN

Hospitality Haunts

You're checked into a charming old inn with a reputation for good food. It's Friday evening, the beginning of a long autumn weekend. A cozy fire is burning gently in the fireplace in your room, and you and your Special One are just settling in front of it, with glasses of pre-dinner champagne. You've got Chopin nocturnes playing softly on the CD player the inn thoughtfully provides. You take off your shoes, put up your feet, stretch, sip, and relax. Life is good. And then you hear a strange noise that seems to come from the closet, but when you check, nothing's there but your clothes. Later, it sounds as though somebody is tapping at your door. When you open it, nobody is in sight. If a few such spooky things happen, do you plan to hightail it out of there first thing in the morning and head for a Holiday Inn, or do you go to dinner grinning big because this is exactly the kind of experience you came for?

There was a time when innkeepers who even thought that they had a ghost in residence tried to keep it secret so

potential guests wouldn't be scared away. And then visiting
haunted inns became trendy enough to deserve space in magazines and newspapers as well as entire guidebooks devoted to
the subject. Stories in newspaper travel sections ran headlines
like ROOMS WITH A BOO. In North Carolina, *Our State* magazine
published a series of stories about inns where earlier occu-
pants never left. Even some Internet sites offer travel guides
for haunted hostelries—telling a little about the nature of the
haunt at each place, and going on to include such details as
amenities, number of rooms, rates, and how to make reserva-
tions. Lots of innkeepers went with the trend. These days,
many old inns use the notion of a ghost on premises as a
marketing tool, perhaps even creating ghosts where none had
been reported before.

In her book *Haunted Inns of the Southeast,* Sheila Turnage
advises prospective guests at such inns to decide ahead of time
just how much ghostly activity they want to experience, and in
each chapter she details those areas in which the most paranormal activity has been reported. "You may want to stay in the
most haunted part of the building, or you may not." Of course
lots of people stay at these inns without ever having heard
the old stories and may leave without experiencing anything
unusual. If you go to an inn hoping to experience its haunting,
are you more likely to encounter a ghost than if you'd gone
uninformed? How much does your imagination have to do with
what happens to you during your stay?

At least three inns in the western North Carolina mountains had stories of the ghostly activity long before it became fashionable to be haunted: Richmond Hill Inn, Balsam Mountain Inn, and Lodge on Lake Lure.

The story of Richmond Hill Inn, in Asheville, is so dramatic it hardly needs ghosts. It started as a private mansion home built 1889, built by the former congressman and diplomat Richmond Pearson and his wife, Gabrielle. It was a lavish showplace meant for elegant entertaining, with plenty of rooms to hold political meetings, serve banquets, and accommodate overnight guests. The mansion had ten fireplaces, soaring ceilings, running water (a rare thing in 1889), and a special elevator just for guests' luggage. Even in the best of its days, though, the place saw tragedy. The Pearsons lost their son to scarlet fever when he was just fourteen years old.

And then as times and fortunes changed, the next generation couldn't afford to live such an expensive way of life, and the building fell into disrepair. Ultimately, the Pearsons' daughter lived there in her old age, in one room, with everything else shut off and deteriorating around her. Just imagining that is pretty ghostly in itself. Since the Pearson heirs didn't want the place, it was scheduled to be torn down, but many local people hated the idea of destroying what had been the finest example of Queen Anne–style architecture in the area. More than once the building got a reprieve as community organizations and the Preservation Society raised money to save the mansion. Albert J. Michel and his wife, Margaret, bought the place in 1987 and had it moved six hundred feet because removing the building from the land on which it stood was a stipulation of the sale. Here's another near-paranormal episode: Imagine moving an old, neglected mansion all in one piece, across rough ground, without it falling apart. Once the building was restored and established as an inn, guests watched a videotape of the tense operation with fascinated disbelief. After the move, bringing the old building back to life involved restoring what could be saved and re-creating what couldn't be restored. Workmen used hand tools rather than electric ones on the woodwork, especially along places such as the staircase banisters, for fidelity to the mansion's original state. Three hundred million dollars later, Richmond Hill Inn opened for guests. The mansion had a dozen guest rooms on the second and third floors. A grand hall, parlor, library, and restaurant, called Gabrielle's in honor of Mrs. Pearson, took up the first floor. Many of Mr. Pearson's own books, some first editions, along with those of North Carolina authors filled the library shelves.

Some of the guest rooms were named for Pearson family members, but the third-floor rooms were named for writers who had ties to North Carolina, with each writer's picture and books included in the room's decor—surely a strong presence.

The inn was expensive but popular, winning many travelers' awards. Additional buildings and a croquet court were added to the inn property, but the history and its ghosts definitely were associated with the mansion. Now that there were guests around to hear them, ghosts became part of the inn's lore. Some people reported hearing the sounds of a ball bouncing and a wagon being pulled across the floor—a memory remnant of the Pearsons' dead son? The F. Scott Fitzgerald room had its share of unexplained phenomena, too, though sometimes he reportedly didn't stay in his room but walked the halls, still handsome and impeccably dressed in an old-fashioned suit.

More disturbing than a fashion plate ghost or a bouncing ball, though, are the associations made with fires at Richmond Hill. In 1948 Fitzgerald's estranged wife, Zelda, died in a fire at the psychiatric hospital in Asheville where she'd been living, off and on, since the early 1930s. The relationship between Scott and Zelda had been stormy and often bitter, complicated by his alcoholism, her mental instability, and their mutual professional jealousy.

The first fire at the refurbished inn occurred in an annex in 1995. The damage was repaired and the place continued in business, with a little speculation about what had caused the fire and, of course, an occasional mention of ghostly influence. But times got tough, with the inn, by now with new management, operating under bankruptcy protection, and on March 19, 2009, fire struck again. This time the damage was huge, destroying Gabriella's Dining Room and much of the mansion. Investigators said arson was the cause. Speculation about supernatural causes increased—Zelda and the fire thing, maybe, or Gabriella not liking what was happening to "her" property, or perhaps just generations of accumulated misery. Local people who had loved the place mourned its destruction, but they didn't all blame paranormal events. One blogger wrote, "Richmond Hill isn't haunted. It just has a lot of history." To be saved from the wrecking ball, moved, enjoy new prosperity, and then be ruined by fire is, indeed, a lot of history. But who knows: Can a ghost start a fire?

Balsam Mountain Inn is another huge rattling, old building rescued by passion, though in this case, it was the determination of a single individual, Merrily Teasley. When she bought the abandoned hotel of more than forty six thousand square feet in 1991, it was in serious disrepair—a place that looked like it should be haunted. Moreover, it stood at 3,500 feet in elevation on a mountainside above the town of Balsam, which had become a ghost town, with boarded-up stores, abandoned vehicles, and wild growth. At that elevation, you can hear the wind blow. In its day this inn had been known as the Grand Old Lady of Balsam, and was a place where families stayed for weeks at a time to escape the heat of Low Country summer. But times change and as the old guests died, new ones did not come along to fill the hotel. Although it was placed on the National Register of Historic Places in 1982, it was not livable and the health department condemned it in 1988. Teasley turned the place around, repairing and restoring the place, laboring side by side with hired workers. She knew what she was doing because she'd already restored another old inn, and she paid close attention to guidelines for historic restoration. By 1991, two floors were livable and up to code, ready for guests. The third floor was ready about a year later. Teasley kept such old touches as claw-foot bathtubs and bead-board walls and, correspondingly, allowed no telephones and no television in guest rooms. And, as you might expect, in all that quietness a new generation of guests began hearing things. Teasley dismissed a story about a local sheriff, shot by a rival for the love of a woman, who wandered the hotel halls, as well as a lady in blue who opened doors and walked through walls. But she said there did seem to be a ghost associated with Room 205, where guests reported responding to a knock on their door several times but never finding anyone there. Another time, guests reported the window in that same room had been raised mysteriously, something a staff person wouldn't do but a ghost might. Apparently this was a friendly ghost. It once gave a woman staying in Room 205 a nice backrub. She'd thought it was her husband, but later realized he wasn't even in the room. Teasley's response to that story was to wish the ghost had made it to her room next. In any case, she always said the resident ghost was friendly.

When Kim and Sharon Shailer took over Balsam Mountain Inn in 2004, they continued the policy of not having television or telephones in the inn's guest rooms, so the absence of those distractions still leaves some guests wondering about strange sounds. The Shailers didn't pay a lot of attention to the ghost stories but did offer another take on what one might hear.

They pointed out that an old wooden structure, with walls of wood and no soundproofing, high in a windy location, "makes its own sounds and transmits the sounds of its guests." A good example is the guest who had stayed at the inn for their monthly "Songwriters in the Round" post-dinner concert in the dining room. Back in her room that night, she heard a cat meowing mournfully over and over and over. As she checked out in the morning, she was just preparing to tell the Shailers the tale of the ghost cat in the next room when the musicians came into the room carrying their guitars and banjos—and a cat in its carrier.

The Lodge on Lake Lure started as another of those places where you could hear through the walls. As former innkeeper Robin Stanier once said, that could get embarrassing, though some guests liked it. Like the tales from Richmond Hill, the story of the ghost at the Lodge on Lake Lure starts with a tragedy, but this one soon becomes lighthearted. The place was built as a getaway for North Carolina highway patrol back in the 1930s. Depending on whose story you believe, it was especially for troopers and their families, or it was for troopers and their fun. One travel writer said, "Everybody knows those guys didn't go up there back then to knit bonnets for their grandmothers. While you're in town, get the old-timers to tell you stories." However things went, one trooper didn't get a lot of play time. Patrolman George Penn was killed in 1937 in a car crash as he was chasing two bad guys through the winding mountain roads. Soon after, if you believe the old tales, he moved into the lodge

permanently, slamming doors, moving things around, and showing himself in the shadows. People who got a glimpse always said
it looked a lot like George. Apparently he hung around even after
the place ceased being a private retreat, passed through the hands
of the Internal Revenue Service, and turned into a bed-and-
breakfast inn open to the public, with Jack and Robin Stanier
becoming the innkeepers in 1990. They turned the spot into a
social gathering place. Guests liked especially to linger around
the great stone fireplace. It has a large millstone centered in the
chimney rock work that sometimes led to speculation about its
significance—how was it possible to get something so heavy up
there and then securely in place? George often came up in the
chatter too, for spiriting the toilet paper out of Room 2, wandering into other guest rooms, walking through closed doors, and
moving items that guests had left lying around. Some people who
claimed to have actually seen a spirit said it looked like a picture
in the house of George Penn. More dramatically, Robin and her
daughter, Betsy, often told the story of the two poltergeist episodes when items flew around as they watched. Once was when
the family was gathering for Christmas dinner, and Robin had
set some prized crystal goblets on the sideboard in honor of the
special occasion. Betsy, Robin, and a friend were checking the
table when Betsy said she wished the ghost would show himself.
In one version of her story, she actually said, "If you're there, give
us a sign." Abruptly, one of the goblets flew from the sideboard
and shattered against a wall across the room. Another time, as

JEANNINE J. WYNNE

George the ghostly patrolman, said to hang around and play jokes here, should be impressed by how the Lodge on Lake Lure has been beautified since the days when it was a simple retreat for highway patrolmen.

Robin was showing the inn to some visitors, or "looky-loos," a flower arrangement in its vase moved off a table and fell to the floor some distance away. Nobody has ever said how the looky-loos reacted. They didn't stay for Christmas dinner, but did they ever come back as guests hoping to meet the ghost?

When the Staniers left innkeeping and sold the inn in 2000, it underwent extensive renovation, which included soundproofing the walls between the rooms and modernizing the bathrooms, as well as upgrading many of the furnishings from casual-cozy and sometimes frankly worn to more elegant comfort. At first the new innkeepers, Giselle Hopke and Mary

Phillips, seemed willing to go along with the notion of George's presence. Mary even claimed that a poltergeist hid things from her. But by the year 2010, not having seen any apparitions, Giselle Hopke admitted they hadn't noticed anything unusual. In the introduction to his book, *Tar Heel Ghosts*, published in 1954, John Harden wrote: "A haunted house needs an old village or town for its locale. Some element of neglect and run-down ruin seems to make an inhabiting ghost more comfortable. Renovation and improvement have been known to rout a well-established specter or scatter a lingering phantom to the four winds." Could it be that after the Lodge on Lake Lure was upgraded to luxury status, George Penn didn't see the fun in soundproof walls and, accustomed to rustic rooms, decided the new digs were too rich for his spirit and moved on?

Also, remembering the days of greater ghostly activity, we have to allow for the Staniers' two big dogs; the golden lab, Muffin, and the black lab, Chip; two lively critters caught more than once chewing a pair of sunglasses or carrying off a watch left on a low table. Who knows what else they might have moved when nobody was looking?

As for Mary's "poltergeist," Giselle said, "Humph. I think she just forgot where she put things."

CHAPTER TWELVE

The Legend of Cowee Tunnel

The Great Smoky Mountains Railroad (GSMR), which is owned by American Heritage Railways, is part of what once was the Murphy Branch of the North Carolina Railroad. The Murphy Branch began in Asheville and gradually extended rails through the mountains to Murphy. Today, the GSMR runs westward from Bryson City to the Nantahala Gorge, and eastward from Bryson City to Dillsboro. On the westward trip, the train rolls along the Tuckasegee River, over the Fontana Lake Trestle, and into the Gorge. If you take the eastward trip, you travel along the Tuckasegee River, through the Cowee Tunnel, and into the village of Dillsboro. The train rides are festive occasions, offering everything from autumn scenic tours and a dinner train to a trip in a private caboose. Dinner events include tasting wine from regional wineries, microbrewery beer tasting, New Year's Eve parties, and mystery theaters.

But the Western North Carolina railway didn't start out as anything remotely pleasant. The history of the railroads in the

North Carolina mountains is long and hard. If you listen closely as you travel east through the Cowee Tunnel, do you hear clanking chains and terrified screams of drowning men? Part of the ride is a recitation of the Legend of Cowee Tunnel.

Convict laborers did much of the construction on the Murphy Branch of the Western North Carolina Railroad. This strenuous work involved laying track on steep grades, building bridges between high peaks, and tunneling through mountain rock. West of Dillsboro, a prison chain gang was ferried on a flatboat from their camp, across the Tuckasegee River, to the worksite. The convicts were shackled together with heavy iron chains and were watched by armed guards as they worked. At the crossing point, the river ran deep, full of strong currents. The date was December 30, 1882, so the mountain water would have been cold, too. A strong rope ran from one side to the other, and the men moved the barge by pulling, hand over hand, on the rope. On the way over, the barge capsized, drowning all aboard except for one unchained trusty, who managed to save the guard. Everyone thought the convict would get a pardon for his heroic act, but he was later convicted of stealing the guard's wallet and sentenced to an additional thirty years of hard labor. The dead convicts were buried in shallow, unmarked graves on a hill near the tunnel, and as you pass through the tunnel, it is said you can still hear the men's frantic cries and the clanking of their chains as they drowned. Can you, really? Wouldn't the sound of train wheels on the tracks inside a tunnel drown out most other sounds? Well, how about an alternate version? Local people outside the tunnel near where the graves are situated report hearing shouts and rattling. But is there truly anything to hear? And what actually happened as the convicts sank into the Tuckasegee River when they tried to ferry across from their camp to the tunnel work site? How many people were on the barge? How many survived? What about the alleged theft? If you were suddenly thrown into an icy, rushing river, trying to stay afloat and save another person at the same time, would you even think of stealing a wallet while you're swimming?

Over time, this story has changed in its details, as legends do, and some people believe that the incident was the culmination of the prisoners' harsh treatment at the time, with drowning being the worst, but not the only, atrocity. And, of course, accounts vary in describing what actually happened. Some popular versions still claim that nineteen chained convicts, a trusty, and a guard were aboard; that nineteen convicts died, with only the trusty and the guard surviving. Older versions of the story, such as the one run by the *Raleigh News and Observer* on January 3, 1883, said twelve of the convicts swam ashore and climbed out of the water, while eighteen others died in chains. By 2005, an account in *The Journal of Appalachian Studies* said nineteen convicts drowned and that Anderson Drake, the convict who saved the guard's life but stole his wallet, received a whipping and a small reward instead of a pardon. The *Journal* said, "Another prisoner, Sam Pickett, saved several men from drowning and was rewarded with a pardon from Governor Jarvis and a gift of $100."

After the disaster, Lieutenant Governor James Robinson went to visit the scene, talking to the officer in charge of the convicts who worked on the Western North Carolina Railroad, and found nothing amiss in how the prisoners had been transported. The chairman of the board of penitentiary directors, Captain E. R. Stamps, also went to the scene of the disaster. In his interpretation, the accident seemed to have been unavoidable because the convicts on the boat, which was in no danger of sinking, panicked when they saw water and ice aboard and ran to one end, capsizing the barge. Many of the convicts could not swim, while those who could were locked in the clutches of the others. Since all were chained together, it's hard to envision any sort of synchronized swim to shore.

According to the Great Smoky Mountains Railroad guidebook *Passage through Time*, it took five hundred convicts, using hand tools and crude explosives created with a mixture of nitroglycerine, sawdust, and cornmeal, then lit with fuses, just to finish the 863-foot Cowee Tunnel. With the hindsight of history, the guidebook said, "Many men lost their lives from sickness and accidents. When the work became miserably hard, some convicts tried to escape, knowing they would be shot in the back." After the accident on the river, the North Carolina House of Representatives asked Stamps to investigate the convict camp. He reported back to Governor Jarvis that no improper conduct had

taken place, adding that the prison diet of "bacon or beef, vegetables, unlimited bread, coffee, and molasses" was satisfactory.
But he acknowledged problems related to scurvy, which comes
from inadequate vitamin C, causing bleeding gums and wounds
that won't heal. In passing the report on to the general assembly,
Governor Jarvis described his policy of treatment for prisoners
as one maintaining a balance. "We did not wish to make the
penitentiary an attractive home or a place of torture. Nor did we
wish to make it a place of idleness or unreasonable labor. Our
policy has been to make every convict who was able to work to
do so; but at the same time to see that he was well clothed, well
fed, and made comfortable."

This brings into question what really was considered
humane treatment of the prisoners who provided cheap labor
to the railroad. North Carolina received a tiny amount, $1.50 a
day, for a virtually unlimited supply of workers. Still, it added
$250,000 a year to the Western North Carolina budget. By the
time construction was complete, more than three thousand five
hundred convicts, nearly all African Americans, had done the
heavy work on the line. At least four hundred and fifty of them
died. Were the demands on the men excessive? As for their diet,
probably the issue of scurvy is not a good measure of treatment,
because some people living free in the mountains also were suf-
fering the lack of fresh fruits and vegetables as a source of vitamin C—they just weren't available. One story from the GSMR
guidebook mentions a situation in which a crew of convicts,

guards, and foremen working during the winter of 1885–1886, camped on the mountain above Murphy. The one hundred fifty men were stranded without supplies by snow, lack of roads, and then, with a thaw, floods. They survived by eating wild game, a diet that couldn't sustain health for very long. Nineteen men died of scurvy before a farmer could haul in supplies with a wagon and oxen. In that situation of shared misery, would the relationships between convicts, foremen, and guards mellow?

The question comes up in yet another story, this one inviting a different interpretation. The Western North Carolina Railroad finally made it to Murphy in 1891, six years late, but an occasion for celebration. The town planned a barbecue in honor of the men who made the final push—convicts included. They sat about, waiting quietly, in groups. Tables to accommodate about one hundred fifty men had been set up, but when it came time for the workers to be seated, local residents pushed in to the tables, triggering a fight, and in the end the workers left without a meal. Would that have happened if the men hadn't been prisoners? Moreover, while the accident that drowned inmates was ghastly, it wasn't the only one associated with the railroad or Cowee Tunnel. In earlier work a section of the tunnel caved in on some of the convicts, though none died.

It was obvious from the time construction began at Asheville in 1880 that laying track from there to Murphy was going to be incredibly difficult. Anyone who has driven any of these mountain roads, even in recent times, will tell you that it's tough to get from one community to another because of narrow roads, hairpin turns, dizzying heights, and precipitous drops—and that's in the day of easy automotive travel. Why would anyone tackle it in the days when the only way to break up a big expanse of rock was by building fires on it to heat it and then dousing the rock with cold water to crack it? The simple answer is commerce.

Asheville had become active in agriculture and was a popular destination for tourists. It was also frequented by loggers and miners who wanted the minerals and timber available in the mountains. And the mountain people certainly wanted their share of such income-producing activity, as well as goods not readily available in their isolated mountain communities. People in the western North Carolina mountains were considered clannish, but that must have been as much a matter of mobility as preference. They could get from one area to another only with great difficulty. According to one old joke, for instance, the only way to get to Boone was to be born there. In this area, the Great Smoky Mountains blocked north and west movement, while the Blue Ridge peaks kept people from moving south, and in the east the Appalachian Highlands were in the way. According to *Passage through Time,* 223 peaks rise above five thousand feet; forty-nine are more than six thousand feet high. Mount Mitchell, in this area, is the highest peak east of the Mississippi. To move beyond your own little area, by foot or pack animal or wagon, took time, energy, a tolerance for risk, and a pressing need. Also, from the perspective of the mountain people, food and supplies from outside became more important after a famine in 1845, when they couldn't grow enough to eat locally and couldn't bring in food from lower areas fast enough to keep it from rotting on the way. It wasn't just food that folks needed. If you lived in the mountains, when an old pot wore out, it might be nice to buy a new one, or to replace worn boots, or buy lamp oil or some fabric. It was just as hard to move anything of value out of the high country as it was to import supplies. Yet these areas were full of trees for timber, such minerals as copper, and gravel and sand for building materials. It was all there. The problem was getting it out to the people who wanted it. Yet the demand was increasing as the state developed. These were the impetus for the ongoing, often ill-fated determination to get rail transportation from Asheville into the western mountains.

Historical accounts of the building process follow the railroad through several changes of ownership, repeated delays, and problems of continuing mishaps, with only a little success at a time, in laying track up steep grades, building trestles, and tunneling into mountain rock.

Even as the challenges were met and trains began to run those rails, it must have seemed as though the Cowee Tunnel was somehow out to get everybody: prisoner, railroad worker, or passenger. It was a hard ride, partly because of the steepness of the mountain grade and because of the nature of the mountain through which the tunnel runs. Balsam Mountain has been described as "crumbly" and "shaky" with unstable soil conditions. Steam engines and diesels sometimes hit rock slides inside the Cowee Tunnel, which brought trains to a thumping halt. Because of the steep grade from Bryson City to Balsam, trains sometimes stalled in the tunnel, leaving the crew in danger from trapped steam and hot smoke. In the late 1960s, a freight train managed to stop just in time to avoid a cave-in. Gradually, however, equipment and the tracks improved and fewer accidents happened even during the years of heaviest use. (Now that the interior of Cowee Tunnel is reinforced with concrete, people ride through it unconcerned.)

It wasn't until 1891 that the Western North Carolina made it to Murphy. Other railroads joined the tracks there, extending service to Georgia, Tennessee, and more areas of North Carolina. For a while, the Murphy Branch thrived, hauling supplies to the little mountain communities and filling the demand elsewhere for timber, pulpwood, and other regional products. The Murphy Branch of the Western North Carolina Railroad brought new businesses, especially tourism, to people living in the western North Carolina mountains. One hotel that became a stopping place for train passengers and crews alike was the Mount Beula Hotel at Dillsboro. A good meal in a comfortable place couldn't miss. In 1894 Frank Jarrett bought the place and named it after himself, Jarrett Springs Hotel. The food, what would be considered good country cooking today, became famous, especially Mr. Jarrett's ham cured by his own unique process. Jarrett House, which was named a National Historic Place in 1984, continues to serve the same hearty fare, including ham, to the raves of people who travel to Dillsboro especially to eat there.

And yet over time the railroad's operation declined almost to the point of extinction. When so many positive things had gone on, what led to its near demise as a business until it was saved as a tourist attraction? Success and progress. Loggers lumbered out the woods faster than nature could replenish them; miners depleted what must have seemed, at first, like inexhaustible ore deposits. The construction of the Fontana Dam in the 1940s created a huge amount of activity for the railroad, but once the dam was built, the demand for hauling diminished along with the population of the temporary Fontana Village, a boomtown that, for a while, was the largest city west of Asheville. When the work was done, the workers left, along with the demand for goods and services and building supplies. Better highways were being built, too, so that traveling by automobile was not a death-defying feat, and people could travel on their personal schedules rather than those of the trains. With little to haul and few passengers to carry, the trains nearly stopped running the Murphy Branch. By 1944, only one passenger train a day made the run. As for freight, the GSMR guidebook, *Passage through Time,* details what happened as the tracks required expensive maintenance at the same time demand for transport declined further when the Champion paper mill in Canton began using wood chips instead of pulpwood. "The tunnels at Dillsboro and Rhodo would not allow high cube woodchip cars

Great Smoky Mountains Railroad preserves a piece of railroading history by keeping trains running for tourists and freight along the Murphy Branch.

COURTESY GREAT SMOKY MOUNTAINS RAILROAD

without extensive work to either lower the roadbed or raise the ceiling. . . . Norfolk Southern filed for abandonment of the western sixty-seven miles between Dillsboro and Murphy in 1988." After that, the North Carolina Department of Transportation bought the line, to preserve it, after no other operators could manage it financially. Several groups cooperated in forming the Great Smoky Mountains Rail*way*, which began improving the tracks and rolling stock, and running excursion trains, attracting tourism to the area once again. On December 23, 1999, American Heritage Railways, which already owned systems in

Colorado, took over, changed the name to Great Smoky Mountains Rail*road,* and expanded the number and variety of excursions. Train rides had become fun, safe, and comfortable. More than two hundred thousand passengers traveled the rails between the Nantahala Gorge, through Bryson City, to Dillsboro each year. Ironically, one factor that contributed to the new success was the very thing that earlier spelled near-disaster—new and improved roads. Interstates and major highways run from major cities such as Atlanta, to the south of Burnsville, and Knoxville to the north. It's a variation on the famous quote from *Field of Dreams,* "Build it and they will come," to a newer version: Restore it, provide easy access, and they will come.

Through all the changing fortunes of the Murphy Branch, the legend of Cowee Tunnel persists. Given the number of disasters and difficulties in the history of the line, why is the Cowee Tunnel, perhaps the most awful of all, the one that has grown to such legendary status that its story is part of pleasure rides on the Great Smoky Mountains Railroad, and appears in nearly all articles about the Murphy Branch?

CHAPTER THIRTEEN

Strange Events at Old Salem

Suppose you're visiting the restored Moravian village, Old Salem, one summer day. As you walk from Winkler's Bakery and turn onto Bank Street, happily chewing on a sweet Love Feast Bun, you step into a spot so cold it seems unnatural. You've just walked into what has become known as "Salem's cold spot." Why is it so cold at the height of summer? The cold patch is beside Vorsteher's House, once the house of the business manager of the Salem Congregation. This brick building is so large that it shades the sidewalk almost all year long. Even in summer, the sun never hits the sidewalk, so no wonder it's cold, the skeptics say. But an old Salem legend amplifies that purely natural explanation with the story of little David.

David was a seven-year-old living in Salem in the early 1900s. After snow fell one January morning, he gathered friends to go sledding. Of course they headed for the steepest hill in Salem, Bank Street. It ran from Church Street down to Main, which unfortunately forms a blind intersection. But kids don't think about things like that. They took turns zipping down the hill until little David hit the intersection just as a streetcar did. The car's motorman, John Ebert, couldn't see David until it was too late to stop. David crashed into the streetcar and was badly injured. Rescuers took David into the Vorsteher's House at the corner of the intersection where doctors did what they could before an ambulance took him to the hospital where he died the same day. The tragedy was made more personal because John Ebert and David were friends who waved to one another every day when the streetcar went past David's house. According to the story, before he died David said he knew that John would never have run over him on purpose. Some people will tell you that spot by the Vorsteher's House is colder than natural, even for a shaded place, because little David's traffic death was the first fatal traffic accident in Salem.

This is just one of many legends that have been passed down over the years in Salem. Strange things that nobody can explain have been happening for a long time. They have been well documented because the Moravians were careful record keepers. Quite apart from the strange events, their meticulous records have made the restoration and re-creation of Old Salem, or Historic Salem, the impressive achievement that it's become. Everything there, from heirloom gardens to crafts and cooking, reflects ongoing study of those old records. The Moravian community became a municipality in 1857, but its history goes back to 1753, when the Moravian Church bought 100,000 acres in the area and named it all "Wachovia." Today that name is widely associated with banking. In the beginning, though, Salem was a church. The church owned all the land and all the residents were part of the church, living in a community run by church committees according to church rules. Imagine the committees of any church you know. What would it be like to live in a town where they handled everything from municipal services and postal delivery to law enforcement and building maintenance? Maybe the amazing thing is that no legends have sprung up around that arrangement.

By 1913, Salem had expanded enough after incorporation to merge with the next town, Winston, where tobacco, not the church, ruled, so Winston-Salem is now the official city name. The Old Salem district went through a period of decline as ongoing development crowded in and the old sites deteriorated. That could have been the end of this historic place if the not-for-profit corporation Old Salem Inc. hadn't formed to protect, restore, and re-create the town. Now it's a thriving center for historic research, museum activities, tourism, and living-history demonstrations. (And the strange happenings, of course.)

The Moravians don't hold with notions of the paranormal, and since continuing history research that keeps Old Salem vibrant depends heavily on Moravian archives, it would be counterproductive to spread stories at odds with Moravian philosophy. So if you ask about unusual events when you visit Old Salem, the stories typically have not mentioned ghosts. This changed a little in 2002 when Moravian archivists published the little book *Ghosts of Salem and Other Tales.* It's based on a folder of articles written by Adelaide L. Fries, archivist and chief historian of the Moravian Church. Her label for the little collection was "Home-made Ghost Stories." When he found this collection, her assistant archivist, Richard Starbuck, decided to add more stories and publish the little book. Despite the ghost of the title, however, each tale ends with a reasonable, not-so-ghostly explanation. So many people bought the book that Old Salem has relented to the point of calling tours to the sites where these things have happened "ghost tours." Tour guides have admitted that it's good for business. But as a marketing director for Old Salem observed, they rely on the documented stories and don't make anything up.

The stories are so much a part of the atmosphere that in the summer young people attending the North Carolina Governor's School at the Salem College campus, a six-week program for intellectually gifted high school students, are offered a "ghost tour" of some of the sites. Here's the summary of his experience by Jackson Boone, who attended the school in 2010. Note its casual tone. "Some of the stories include a ghost of a little girl who died in the elevator of Clewell dormitory who still haunts it. Also, a painting of Mary Babcock in the Babcock dorm has been known to stare at those who dishonor her painting. The Single Sisters' and Single Brothers' houses both have been known to have apparitions of uneasy souls who want to find partners. Finally, the cemetery near one of the old Moravian churches has

STRANGE EVENTS AT OLD SALEM

a slave burial ground in which some claim to have seen ghosts dancing on the 'Teenth of June' (I'm not sure what that meant)."

It's odd that these summer students stay in a dormitory at Salem College, which is mainly a school for women. One promotional note says that women go to college to find husbands, but they go to Salem College to find bridesmaids. Apparently the female experience really has been different than that of males. A janitor at the school has said the dormitories are associated with such scary stories that some of the girls are afraid to go out alone at night. As recently as 2010, some young women were reporting episodes of odd sounds at windows and "felt" presences, so much so that friends avoided some of their rooms. But Jackson never mentioned any such sense.

Nor does he mention the story most often told on tours and in print, about the Little Red Man who used to appear at the Single Brothers' House. It goes back to the days when an excavation for the Single Brothers' House caved in on some of the workers as they were digging a basement for an addition to the building. Andreas Kremser, a single brother and a shoemaker, died in the collapse on March 26, 1786. Reportedly, he was a small man wearing red—a jacket or a hat, depending on who tells the story—at the time of the accident. Adelaide Fries wrote about the incident in 1934, basing her account on the official record of his death in the Church Book of Salem Congregation. The brothers were hollowing out a soil bank from one side, and Kremser was kneeling as he dug. About midnight, one of the brothers noticed that the bank was falling in and he yelled to everyone to jump away. The others got out more or less unscathed, but Kremser couldn't move fast enough because he'd been working on his knees. As Fries described it, "He was covered by the falling dirt and quite buried alive." They got him out, still alive and talking, but he died just a couple of hours later. They buried him on the 27th in the God's Acre cemetery. Nobody has ever mentioned sensing his presence in the cemetery. Records imply that he'd been unusually quiet all day before his death and seem to suggest that his kneeling position as he dug was prayerful, that he was ready to go to his final rest.

But for a time, he was reported being all over the Single Brothers' House, first by the brothers, later by a child, and later still by a visiting citizen of good standing. The earliest stories were about odd sounds—unexplained tapping, usually at night, that could be interpreted as the sound of a shoemaker's hammer. When they heard it, the brothers would reassure one another, "There's Kremser." Occasionally someone would claim to hear footsteps in the hall and see a little man in red scurry past a doorway.

In time, older women took over the building from the single brothers, and a child visiting her grandmother claimed that a little man invited her to play. More such stories followed but were generally dismissed by folks in the community—"You know how strange elderly women can get." A visitor from nearby changed that when he went to the house to inspect the way subcellars were constructed, and was shown around by "one of the substantial citizens of Salem," as Fries put it. As the substantial citizen told the Kremser story to the visitor, the Little Red Man appeared, grinning, and then adroitly eluded attempts by the two men to catch him. They reached out to nothing but empty air. These days, wouldn't you wonder what substance was influencing the men's perceptions? In this case, Fries capitulates on her position of perfectly natural explanations for what happens. "Incidentally, I might remark that the aforesaid substantial citizen was *not* addicted to the use of spirituous refreshments, so that otherwise obvious explanation will not suffice." Eventually a minister performed an exorcism, ordering the Little Red Man to "go to rest." After that, he wasn't seen again, at least not right away. Fries wrote almost sadly that this was the "most long-lived ghost that Salem has owned," but then she can't resist some final no-nonsense words: "it seems an open question whether one should be grateful to the clergyman who exorcised him, or to the electric lights which have driven the shadows from the subcellars of the one-time Brothers' House." Still, folks can't quite let him go, especially around Halloween, when they're looking for something spooky. A man who was playing the role of Brother Kremser as part of Halloween tours, including the cellar of the house, wore a red hat for the role. When he was alone there between tours, he said he heard something or somebody tap-tap-tapping. Was it that shoemaker, Kremser, back again?

If he was, he might not have been alone. Some people who have worked at Old Salem in recent years claim they've had odd experiences that suggest other presences, some centered in the Old Salem bookstore when it was still located in a house built by John Christian Blum, who printed the town's first newspaper. His press was still there. In 2005 Phoebe Zerwick wrote a story for the *Winston-Salem Journal* newspaper describing her visit to Old Salem. Her report included the familiar stories, such as the Little Red Man, but then moved on to more recent happenings in the Blum House and bookstore.

Tracy Jacobus was managing the store and started having odd experiences almost as soon as she started work there a couple of years earlier. She said she didn't tell anybody at first because as the daughter of a psychic she'd been reluctant to discuss unusual things that happened lest people think she was a little crazy. At first she just heard footsteps overhead and conversations in other rooms when she knew the house was empty. It wouldn't be too hard to keep quiet about that. But that changed the day she looked up from where she was sitting on the stairs into the press room. She said she saw a man in early-nineteenth-century clothing wearing the kind of leather apron printers wore. And this ghost looked right at her. She stared back. She thought each of them was challenging the right of the other to be there. What kind of a confrontation would have ensued if they'd continued? Ah, but saved by the bell. It rang when a customer opened the door to come into the shop. By the time Jacobs had greeted her customer and turned back, the man in the apron was gone. She finally started asking colleagues if they'd had any odd experiences, to which one woman replied that she'd seen a person standing by the press, while another said she'd never actually seen anyone but had heard someone walking around upstairs. Then in the summer of 2005, people upstairs in their offices before the shop opened heard sounds below. When they hurried down to investigate, the door was still locked and the shop empty. After that, the front door to the store kept locking itself, the back door opened when nobody was there, and footsteps echoed from supposedly empty rooms. The folks making these observations weren't sure the presence was Blum or, if it was, why he was hanging around, because although he did have a run of bad luck and ended up with heavy debt, it didn't seem like the sort of thing that would make a man stay past his time. But even the skeptics agreed that they'd heard sounds in the house that nobody could explain.

By the summer of 2010, though, things seemed to have calmed down. The bookstore had already moved to a new location, and Blum's old building became home to an exhibit on printing featuring his press and displays of Old Salem photography as it has evolved from the earliest years. Paula Locklair, vice president for education at Old Salem, said people still occupy offices upstairs in the Blum House, but if anybody has experienced anything unusual, they haven't talked about it. Still, she offered to ask around and call back if she learned anything new. She didn't call.

If it seems that spirits need a building or graveyard to manifest, ordinary legends don't. It's hard to know how one gets started, and it's fascinating to see how it grows and morphs. One of the most famous legends in Old Salem isn't ghostly at all. And it's been a topic of conversation since 1803—the big coffeepot standing at Main Street and Brookstown Avenue. The thing measures more than seven feet tall and is supposed to be big enough to hold seven hundred and forty gallons of coffee. Since it is sixteen feet around, just how you'd pour from it isn't clear. Moreover, since the bottom was constructed with an open space, liquid would've run out as fast as it was put in. That scotches the popular story that the pot was used to serve large groups of Moravians during Love Feasts.

The story of how the tin pot came to exist at all goes back to 1858, when a tinsmith, Julius Mickey, opened a grocery store on a lot at the southwest corner of Main and Belews Streets. He intended the grocery store to be his livelihood, but since there was extra space in his building, he started a tin shop, too. In those years people used tin for plates, cups, pans, buckets, dippers, and most other kitchen and dining ware. Mickey apparently was a good tinsmith in the right place at the right time, because the tin business took off, outstripping his food store. Success attracts imitators. A competitor went into business down the street and tried to lure Mickey's potential customers into his own shop before they realized his stuff was a knockoff. Mickey took care of that by building his huge tin coffeepot so it would be obvious to all where his shop stood. Mickey put the massive pot up on a pole by the street in front of his store, identifying *his* place as the real, original tinsmith shop. It must have worked, because he continued in business until his death, when another tinsmith, L.B. Brickenstein, took over his shop, keeping the coffeepot in place. But even in those slower times, anything mounted too close to a road could create a hazard. According to the old records, teams of horses sometimes ran into the post, which wasn't good for the pot or the horses. Then in 1920 a driver in a motorcar going at least twenty miles per hour hit the post and knocked the pot onto the sidewalk, where it almost hit a woman and child. The near-disaster led the Winston-Salem aldermen to forbid putting the pot, which must have been pretty beat up by then anyhow, back onto its post. Not only was it dangerous, they said, but it also went against local laws limiting advertising signs. That might have been the end of it had not the Wachovia Historical Society and a Moravian bishop made a fuss about preserving the artifact. The aldermen capitulated, but said the coffeepot had to be farther from the street. After that, all was calm until construction of Interstate 40 was planned on a route that would have run directly over the pot. Since the engineers wouldn't bend the highway, there was nothing to do but move the coffeepot, which by then had come to stand as a symbol of Winston-Salem generally and Old Salem in particular. Town officials moved the pot out of the way of interstate progress in 1959 to where the bypass for Old Salem meets Main Street. It has stood there ever since and figures visually in much of Old Salem's promotional material. All this information was gleaned from town records by *Winston-Salem Journal and Sentinel* reporter Chester Davis. His

The huge coffee pot towering over the landscape has become Salem's
identifying landmark. It was made in 1859 by the tinsmiths Julius and Samuel
Mickey and is commonly called "The Mickey Pot."

story appeared in the paper's Bicentennial Edition, April 10, 1996. Any reporter who was working during this era can tell you that bicentennial stories went into way more detail than usual newspaper stories partly because the Bicentennial Beast had to be fed and it took many words to keep it going.

The legends that have grown around the pot, however, wouldn't have passed any contemporary newspaper editor's hairy eyeball except as part of a special story. For sheer indignation, you can't beat archivist Adelaide Fries's 1934 observations: "At just what period in its history the traditions began I cannot say, but schoolchildren and newspaper reporters combine in perpetuating them and in adding to their inaccuracy." One legend holds that a Revolutionary spy hid in the pot, another that it was used as a mail-drop for a British spy, still another that General Cornwallis and his troops stayed there because there was no place in town. But Fries wrote, "The Coffee Pot did not exist in the days of the Revolution, and no army could shelter in its space, which could hardly accommodate one grown man." And, of course, you can't make coffee in a pot with a false bottom. A couple of stories about the pranks of kids trying to blow the thing up with a homemade firecracker are true. So is the earlier one about boys hiding inside and scaring visitors by yelling through the spout. Above all, because the coffeepot has come to stand for Salem, visitors and local folks expect to see it there. They'll probably believe some of the legends they've heard, and once they're wandering about in Old Salem, who knows what else will happen?

CHAPTER FOURTEEN

The Spirits of Salisbury

People in Salisbury think it's a great place to live. The population usually hovers at around thirty thousand people—a smallish place. But it's only thirty-some miles from the bigger cities, Charlotte and Winston-Salem, should one need a city fix. Salisbury has a symphony orchestra, two colleges, an excellent library, a visual arts center with a scent garden, an active community theater, a couple of wine shops, a variety of nice restaurants, several coffeehouses, lots of decent lunch places, an independent bookstore, greenways and bike paths, a long-established newspaper, an active historic preservation society, and lots of museums and historic sites to visit. Many residents boast that they can walk to work as well as to most of the other places they want to go. The surrounding countryside in Rowan County includes a winery and several farms that offer their products at the downtown farmers' market. Why would anyone want to leave? Maybe some don't— not ever.

One tourism brochure for the area uses the motto "Where the past is still present." No doubt they were referring to the availability of historic sites and tours in the area, but it seems that a goodly number of people from earlier years don't even want to leave after their time has come and gone. They're still around. The community has so many ghosts and apparitions and spirit episodes the place is beginning to seem crowded. If you can't beat 'em, join 'em. Ghost tours of some "haunted" properties have become a regular feature of local activity, often starting at the Wrenn House, a popular restaurant for lunch meetings, dinner, and special occasions. The Wrenn House has been reporting strange activity for a long time, with much of it presumably dating back to the era when it was an academy for children.

It's the staff and the owner, Michael Morefield, who have had the experiences, not guests. They've heard piano music coming from an upstairs room where a piano once stood. Sometimes they hear small children laughing. Morefield once walked into a room and saw a little girl sitting on a barstool. She disappeared as soon as he entered. In other activity, the staff said that after they set up a room for a banquet at the end of a workday, they came back in the morning to find all their work undone, with the table settings on the floor and the chairs on the table. The house was built in 1839, but it's had so many additions over the years that dating is uncertain, and it could be even older. The old structures around Salisbury are the ones that seem to have the most unexplained activity.

You can see why the city's people might have reported all kinds of spooky activity over the years: The area is rich in the kinds of history that spawn such stories. During the Revolutionary War, British General Cornwallis and his troops occupied the town for a couple of days. During the Civil War, Confederate activity was strong here because the town was at the point where east-west and north-south rail lines met. A prison for Union soldiers was established in an old yarn mill. Before the war was over, 11,700 of them had died and were buried in mass graves. They were memorialized at that site, named the Salisbury National Cemetery by the United States government in 1874. In 1907 five local manufacturing plants burned down at a place near the Old Lutheran Cemetery where several hundred Confederate soldiers were buried. And the Rowan County Administration Building, directly across from the building that houses the Salisbury Post Offices and presses, has a long history, first as a federal courthouse, then a United States post office. People tell stories about strange experiences associated with all these places, ranging from occasional modern photographs of the Lutheran Cemetery in which flames seemed to burn behind the gravestones to people seeing apparitions in the basement of the Administration Building. But the sites that have reported the most frequent ongoing activity in the late twentieth and early twenty-first centuries have been right in the heart of Salisbury's downtown, that area where locals gloat over being able to walk to everything. The Wrenn House is just at the fringe of the area. Other vivid, ongoing accounts have involved restaurants smack in the center of downtown. Why would spirits want to hang around eating places? Disembodied presences don't need food, do they?

Odd things had been going on at The Brick Street Tavern even before it opened under that name. When she was a student, Daphne Safrit worked at the restaurant while it was Las Palmos. Now a college graduate with a degree in anthropology, Daphne manages the Literary Bookpost on Main Street, just a couple of blocks away. She recounted some of the things that happened to her and other employees while they worked at Las Palmos. Sometimes it was just a feeling of unease or having been touched when nobody was near, but other times, items that the staff left in one place were found later in another, with everybody claiming not to have moved anything. Daphne recalled leaving many boxes inside an upstairs room with a door that opened inward. Next day, when she tried to go into the room, the door wouldn't budge, because all the boxes had been pushed up hard against it. What mystified her was that nobody could have come out through the door after buttressing it, and there was no other way in or out of that room, not even a dropped ceiling.

One of her most compelling stories was about the time a colleague came down from the mezzanine in the building pale and trembling. She asked him what was wrong. "I just saw a woman up there," he said. "She walked through the wall and disappeared." It got so employees wouldn't stay alone in the place after hours. Later, after Las Palmos closed for good, three people were cleaning up the third floor of the old building when one of them walked smack into a solid but invisible wall. "You couldn't see the wall," Daphne said, "but you could see its shadow on the floor."

Could the wall have been some sort of spirit memory from an earlier time in the building? Las Palmos opened in 1987, but the whole building was built in 1906 by Victor Wallace and Sons to create space for their expanding dry goods business. Additions were built later, and a sewing machine factory was established on the second floor. A pool hall, the Friendly Cue, operated for twenty years in the same building. It moved across the street when Las Palmos moved in and has done business from there ever since. Stories haven't circulated about anything unusual happening at the Friendly Cue's new digs.

But happenings have been so frequent and dramatic at the Brick Street Tavern that the owner, John Casey, invited the Salisbury Paranormal Investigations group to study the restaurant. This is a volunteer group that investigates for free. One of its members became involved because of strange happenings in her own home. While ghost tours are mostly for fun, this group has tried to bring scientific examination to bear, operating with the motto "Sometimes people just want to know the truth." The investigators' approach has been systematic. Working with microphones, recorders, cameras, and devices to measure electromagnetic activity, the group documents everything from date and time of each investigation to room temperature, as well as what happened as they walked through the site. At the Brick Street Tavern, all the team members reported their hair standing on end, "including the male's hair on his legs." Their videos show what they believe is a solid form walking past a third-floor window in the rear of the warehouse, as well as their own shadows, which are translucent, not solid. In recording their attempts to engage entities in conversation at the Brick Street Tavern, the team said they made out several different dialects, including African-American and Scotch-Irish, two ethnic groups strongly represented in Salisbury at the turn of the century. They speculate that the African-American man could have been a Wallace family employee who worked as a freight elevator operator in the family's dry goods business. On their audio recording, team comments made trying to engage the entities in conversation are clear. The responses are muffled. The investigators offer translation, but while some people could see what's in the pictures, they were skeptical about the sound recordings. Many, including Daphne Safrit, did hear something but couldn't make out any words. She said a group of friends listening with her suggested slowing down the playback to listen again. One of them translated, "Sam is sexy."

"But since his name is Sam," Daphne said, "I don't think I believed him."

The Salisbury Paranormal team learned in their research that transient people had used the warehouse section of the building as a shelter for years. Their report says, "Quite possibly they remain here, as they have nowhere else to go."

Were they tired of being pestered? After the serious investigations began, unexplained activity at both Brick Street Tavern and Wrenn House increased and it seemed unfriendly. Some people have been injured as they worked. One woman fell down the stairs. (Well, that does happen, doesn't it?) Daphne said she had never been afraid of what happened when she worked at Las Palmos, but she wouldn't want to go back to Brick Street Tavern. "I think we should just leave them alone. Investigators are making them mad," she said.

Or maybe the place is just filling up. Shortly after the 2010 investigation, a kitchen worker at Cartucci's Italian Restaurant across the street from the Brick House Tavern started talking about a ghost in the kitchen. Her English was limited, so it wasn't clear whether she said it hit her in the head with a cookie sheet or with a pan, but she was scared. If the spirits won't leave, she might! At least that would reduce the local population by one.

BIBLIOGRAPHY

The Lost Colony

Campbell, Elizabeth A. *The Carving on the Tree.* Boston, Massachusetts: Little, Brown and Company, 1968.

Clark, Josh. "What happened to the lost colony at Roanoke?" http://history.howstuffworks.com/american-history/roanoke-colony1.htm (accessed February 24, 2010).

Estes, Roberta. "The Story of Roanoke, Sir Walter Raleigh's Lost Colony." The Lost Colony Genealogy and DNA Research Group, www.rootsweb.ancestry.com/~molcgdrg /faqs/lcstory.htm (accessed February 26, 2010).

Harrington, J.C. *Archaeology and the Enigma of Fort Raleigh.* Raleigh, North Carolina: Division of Archives and History, North Carolina Department of Cultural Resources, 1984.

Hauser, Eric. "The Lost Colony: Roanoke Island, NC." www .coastalguide.com/packet/lostcolony-croatan.shtml (accessed February 24, 2010).

Miller, Helen Hill. *Passage to America.* Raleigh, North Carolina: Division of Archives and History, North Carolina Department of Cultural Resources, 1983.

Odrowaz-Sypniewska, Margaret, B.F.A. "Roanoke Island, the Virginian Colony (now in North Carolina)." www .courtlylives.com/Roanoke.html (accessed February 24, 2010).

Quinn, David B. and Alison M., eds. *The First Colonists: Documents on the Planting of the First English Settlements in North America 1584–1590*. Raleigh, North Carolina: Division of Archives and History, Department of Cultural Resources, 1982.

"Roanoke Colony," http://en.wikipedia.org/wiki/Roanoke_ Colony (accessed February 18, 2010).

Wetmore, Ruth Y. *First on the Land: The North Carolina Indians.* Winston-Salem, North Carolina: John F. Blair, Publisher, 1985.

Willard, Fred. "Raleigh's 1587 Lost Colony: Conspiracy, Spies, Secrets & Lies." www.lost-colony.com/currentresearch.html (accessed February 28, 2010).

Historic Gold Hill

Harden, John. *Tar Heel Ghosts.* Chapel Hill: The University of North Carolina Press, 1954.

Historic Gold Hill, regular visits by author, 1990–2010.

McCullough, Gary L. *North Carolina's State Historic Sites.* Winston-Salem, North Carolina: John F. Blair, Publisher, 2001.

Pennington-Hopkins, Vivian. *Gold Hill Ghosts and Other Legends.* Gold Hill, North Carolina: Historic Gold Hill and Mines Foundation, Inc., 2009.

―――. Telephone interview by author, May 27, 2010.

Pitzer, Sara. *North Carolina off the Beaten Path—Ninth edition.* Guilford, Connecticut: The Globe Pequot Press, 2009.

Roberts, Nancy. *The Gold Seekers: Gold, Ghosts, and Legends from Carolina to California.* Columbia: The University of South Carolina Press, 1989.

www.historicgoldhill.com

www.reedmine.com

Pee Dee A.D.

Boudreaux, Edmond A. *The Archaeology of Town Creek.* Tuscaloosa, Alabama: The University of Alabama Press, 2007.

Coe, Joffre Lanning. *Town Creek Indian Mound: A Native American Legacy.* Chapel Hill, North Carolina, and London, England: University of North Carolina Press, 1995.

"NC Historic Sites – Town Creek Indian Mound." www
.nchistoricsites.org (accessed April 16, 2010, and May 2,
2010).

"Town Creek Indian Mound," http://en.wikipedia.org/wiki
/Town_Creek_Indian_Mound (accessed May 2, 2010).

"Town Creek Indian Mound" (NC Historic Site). www
.learnnc.org/lp/pages/2167 (accessed May 2, 2010).

"Town Creek Indian Mound: Clays of the Piedmont. www
.learnnc.org/lp/editions/cede_piedclay/235 (accessed May 2,
2010).

www.myfox8.com/news/cheaptrips/wgbh-cheap-trips-indian-
mound-090423,0,2853668.story (accessed May 2, 2010).

Tsul 'Kalu and the Judaculla Rock

"Judaculla Rock." eSlacklish, updated by M. Rebekah Otto,
Annetta.

http://atlasobscura.com/place/judaculla-rock (accessed March 1,
2010).

Priestley, Kent. "Rock of Ages." *Western North Carolina
Magazine*, January 2009.

Setzer, Lynn. "Once Upon a Time." *Raleigh News and Observer*. www.mountainlovers.com (accessed March 2, 2010).

"The Slant-Eyed Giant." www.firstpeople.us/FP-Htmle-Legends/TheSlant-eyedGiant-Cherokee.html (accessed March 4, 2010).

"The Stories on the Rock." gulahiyi.blogspot.com/2009/02/stories-on-rock.html (accessed March 4, 2010).

"Tsul 'Kalu." http://en.wikipedia.org/wiki/Tsul_'Kalu (accessed March 1, 2010).

The Sad Tale of Tom Dula

Holt, David. "Tom Dula's Grave." www.davidholt.com/photos/tomdula.html (accessed March 22, 2010).

http://en.wikipedia.org/wiki/Tom_Dula.

McClung, Marshall. "Dooley Legend Lives as Group Seeks Pardon." www.main.nc.us/graham/mcclung/Dooley%20Legend.html (accessed March 22, 2010).

McCrumb, Sharyn. "Tom Dooley: Bound to Die." January 30, 2009. www.blueridgecountry.com/archive/tom-dooley.html (accessed March 9, 2010).

Reynolds, Karen. Telephone interview by the author. Wilkes County, March 19, 2010.

Sanders, Craig. "The True Story of Tom Dooley." November 1, 2008. www.suite101.com/traditional-folk-music .article,cfm/the_true_story_of ... (accessed February 28, 2010).

West, John Foster. *The Ballad of Tom Dula*. Durham, North Carolina: Moore Publishing Company, 197–.

_____. *Lift up Your Head, Tom Dooley*. Asheboro, North Carolina: Down Home Press, 1993.

www.wilkesplaymakers.com/contente.asp?page _id=dooleye (accessed March 9, 2010).

Blackbeard the Pirate

"Blackbeard." www.wikipedia.org/wiki/Blackbeard (accessed December 22, 2009).

Duffus, Kevin P. *The Last Days of Black Beard the Pirate*. Raleigh, North Carolina: Looking Glass Productions, Inc., 2008.

Konstam, Angus. *Blackbeard: America's Most Notorious Pirate*. Hoboken, New Jersey: John Wiley and Sons, 2006.

Lee, Robert E. *Blackbeard the Pirate: A Reappraisal of His Life and Times*. Winston-Salem, North Carolina: John F. Blair, Publisher, 1974.

QAR. www.qaronline.org (accessed January 2, 2009).

Rankin, Hugh F. *The Pirates of Colonial North Carolina.* Raleigh, North Carolina: State Department of Archives and History, 1960.

Whedbee, Charles Harry. *Blackbeard's Cup and Stories of the Outer Banks.* Winston-Salem, North Carolina: John F. Blair, Publisher, 1989.

———. *Legends of the Outer Banks and Tar Heel Tidewater.* Winston-Salem, North Carolina: John F. Blair, Publisher, 1966.

www.ocracoke-nc.com/blackbeard (accessed January 5, 2009).

Brown Mountain Lights

"Brown Mountain Lights." www.westernncattractions.com /BMLights.htm (accessed November 15, 2009).

"Brown Mountain Lights, The." Unexplained America. www .prairieghosts.com/brownmtn.html (accessed November 15, 2009).

"Brown Mountain Lights Myths and Legends." www.dancaton .physics.appstate.edu/BML/Legends (accessed November 15, 2009).

Charlotte Observer 1924 Article on the Brown Mountain Lights www.dancaton.physics.appstate.edu/BML/CharObs092413 .htm (accessed November 15, 2009).

"History of the Brown Mountain Lights." www.dancaton .physics.appstate.edu/BML/History/ (accessed April 7, 2010).

"Overlook's Makeover Unveiled." Sharon McBrayer. *The News Herald.* www2.morganton.com/news/2009/sep/02 /overlooks-makeover-unveiled-ar-b6043/ (accessed November 15, 2009).

Roberts, Nancy. *Southern Ghosts.* Garden City, New York: Doubleday and Company, Inc., 1979.

USGS Report. www1.appstate.edu/dept/physics/canton/BML /index.htm (accessed April 7, 2010).

Apparition at Maco Station

Harden, John. *Tar Heel Ghosts.* Chapel Hill, North Carolina: The University of North Carolina Press, 1954.

Howell, Edward. Telephone interview by author. May 15, 2010.

———. E-mails to author. May 6, 8, 9, 10, 2010.

"The Light at Maco Station." Jim Hall. www.hauntednc.com /legends_maco.htm (accessed April 29, 2010).

"Maco Light." http://en.wikipedia.org/w/index.php?title= Maco_light&printable=yes.

———. NC HAGS Paranormal Observers. "Maco Light Investigation #2," www.youtube.com, June 26, 2007 (accessed May 8, 2010).

———. NC HAGS Paranormal Observers. "Maco Light Special Edition," remastered, www.youtube.com, January 3, 2010 (accessed May 8, 2010).

The Devil's Tramping Ground

Bryan, Bobette. "The Devil's Stomping Grounds." www .underworldtales.com/devil.htm (accessed November 17, 2009).

Chase, Tom. "Valujet Plane Crash in Florida, One Year Later." Tom Chase. www.zodiacal.com/articles/chase/valujet.php (accessed January 25, 2010).

Crane, Jon L. e-mail to the author, February 10, 2010.

"Devil's Stomping Ground." www.hauntspot.com/haunt/usa /north-carolina/devils-stomping-shtml (accessed November 17, 2009).

Fields, Janis. "The Devils Tramping Ground." www .essortment.com/all/devilstramping_rgkt.htm (accessed November 17, 2009).

Harden, John. *The Devil's Tramping Ground: and Other North Carolina Mystery Stories.* Chapel Hill: The University of North Carolina Press, 1948.

Harrington, Kady. "The Devil's Tramping Ground." www
.hauntednc.com/legends_dtg.htm (accessed January 25,
2010).

The Ballad of Frankie Silver

Avery, K. Clinton (compiled and edited). *Official Court Record
of the Trial, Conviction and Execution of Francis Silvers—First
Woman Hanged in North Carolina—From the Minutes of the
Burke County Superior Court,* Morganton, North Carolina:
The News-Herald, 1969.

"Frankie Silver: They Won't Hang a Woman." North
Carolina Cultural Resources Newsroom. http://news.ncdcr
.gov/2008/12/04/frankie-silver-they-won't-hang-a-woman/
(accessed March 25, 2010).

Harbin, Jim. *Nancy's Story: To Right the Legend of Frankie
Silver.* Maggie Valley, North Carolina: Ravenscroft
Publishing, 2000.

McCrumb, Sharyn. *The Ballad of Frankie Silver.* New York,
New York: Dutton, 1998.

Patterson, Beverly. *"Give Me the Truth!": The Frankie Silver
Story in Contemporary North Carolina.* www.folkstreams.net
/context,160 (accessed April 16, 2010).

Phillips, Theresa. Telephone interview by author, May 25,
2010.

Whited, Lana. Ferrum College. *Using The Ballad of Frankie Silver to Teach the Conventions of Narrative.* Paper presented at the September 2000 Appalachian Teachers' Network Conference, Radford University. www.ferrum.edu/applit /articles/truestory.htm (accessed March 25, 2010).

Young, Perry Deane. *The Untold Story of Frankie Silver.* Asheboro, North Carolina: Down Home Press, 1998.

Hospitality Haunts

Harden, John. *Tar Heel Ghosts.* Chapel Hill, North Carolina: The University of North Carolina Press, 1954.

Hopke, Giselle. Telephone interview by author, May 5, 2010.

Jackson, L. A. "Hauntings in the Hills." *Our State* magazine, October 2004, pp. 170–177.

Jackson, L. A.; Gissna, Bill; Sullivan, Lisa. "Inns." *Our State* magazine, October 2008, pp. 102–104.

Pitzer, Sara. *Off the Beaten Path: North Carolina: Seventh Edition.* Guilford, Connecticut: The Globe Pequot Press, 2005.

———. *Recommended County Inns of the South—Sixth Edition.* Old Saybrook, Connecticut: The Globe Pequot Press, 1997.

"Richmond Hill Inn." http://en.wikipedia.org/wiki/Richmond_ Hill_Inn (accessed September 30, 2010).

Stanier, Robin. Conversation with author, Lake Lure, July 1997.

Turnage, Sheila. *Haunted Inns of the Southeast.* Winston-Salem, North Carolina: John F. Blair, Publisher, 2001.

Welcome Book. www.balsaminn.com/roombook.htm (accessed May 25, 2010).

"Zelda Fitzgerald." http://en.wikipedia.org/wiki/Zelda_Fitzgerald (accessed May 20, 2010).

The Legend of Cowee Tunnel

"All Aboard: Official Publication of the Great Smoky Mountains Railroad." 2010. (No other publication data provided.)

"An awful accident/eighteen convicts drowned at once/a flat boat sinks with them in the Tuckaseegee River." *The Raleigh News and Observer.* January 3, 1883.

"Back of Beyond," DVD provided by the Great Smoky Mountains Railroad. 2010.

Carson III, Homer S. "Penal Reform and Construction of the Western North Carolina Railroad, 1875–1892." *Journal of Appalachian Studies*, Spring–Fall 2005, vol. 11, no. 1–2, pp. 205–225.

Craft Revival: "Shaping Western North Carolina Past and Present." www.wcu.edu/craftrevival/story/train/1890s /1890dillsboro.html (accessed November 20, 2009).

George, Michael and Strack, Frank. *Passage through Time: The Official Guidebook.* 2000. (No other publication data in the book.)

Osment, Timothy N. "Railroads in Western North Carolina." www.learnnc.org/1p/editions/nchist=newsouth/5503 (accessed April 29, 2010).

www.gsmr.com/about/history.php

Strange Events at Old Salem

Boone, Jackson. E-mail to author, June 29, 2010.

Davis, Chester. "The Coffee Pot." *Winston-Salem Journal and Sentinel,* April 10, 1966. www.fmoran.com/cofftxt.html (accessed July 1, 2010).

Locklair, Paula. Telephone interview with author, July 1, 2010.

Roberts, Nancy. *North Carolina Ghosts and Legends.* Columbia: University of South Carolina Press, 1991.

Starbuck, Richard (compiler). *Ghosts of Salem and Other Tales.* Winston-Salem, North Carolina, 2002.

Zerwick, Phoebe. "Winston-Salem: The Ghosts of Historic Old Salem District." *Winston-Salem Journal,* November 1, 2005. www.skyscrapercity.com/showthread.php?t=275984 (accessed June 9, 2010).

The Spirits of Salisbury

Potts, Shavonne. "Food, entertainment on tap at Brick Street Tavern." *Salisbury Post*, April 15, 2009.

Rowan County Tourism Development Authority. *Historic Salisbury, Rowan County, North Carolina*, brochure, 2003.

Safrit, Daphne. Interviews with author, 2009 to July 3, 2010.

Salisbury, North Carolina: Self-published, 2003.

Salisbury History and Art Trail, brochure, 2010.

Scarvey, Katie. "Downtown Salisbury Ghost Walk starts Friday." *Salisbury Post*, April 14, 2010.

Sides, Susan Goodman. *Historic Salisbury and Rowan County in Vintage Postcards*. Salisbury, North Carolina: Self published, 2003.

www.salisburyparanormal.com/investigations.html (accessed July 2, 2010).

INDEX

ABOUT THE AUTHOR

Sara Pitzer has published books about travel and food and is the author of *North Carolina off the Beaten Path*, also published by Globe Pequot Press. Sara has written for *Our State Magazine*, worked on the staff of the *Salisbury Post*, and provided travel stories and weekly columns for the *Charlotte Observer*. Sara has received the Charles Kurault award from the North Carolina Travel Industry Association. She lives in the Piedmont region of the state.